FOR MYP 4

Personal Project

Skills for Success

Laura England
Angela Stancar Johnson

FOR MYP 4&5

Personal Project

Skills for Success

Laura England
Angela Stancar Johnson

HODDER EDUCATION

The Publishers would like to thank the following for permission to reproduce copyright material.

Photo credits

pp. vi-1, 8-9, 26-27, 40, 59, 70, 75, 86-87, 90, 93 © Tabthipwatthana/stock.adobe.com, **p.33** *top to bottom* © jovannig/stock.Adobe.com, © Herman/stock.Adobe.com, © bst2012/stock.Adobe.com, © Marek/stock.Adobe.com, © Richard Carey/stock.Adobe.com, © PixieMe/stock.Adobe.com

Acknowledgements

The authors would like to acknowledge Good Shepherd Lutheran College and Southbank International School for some of the student resources used.

Bibliography

International Baccalaureate Organization, *IB Middle Years Programme Projects guide*, 2014, Geneva, Switzerland, International Baccalaureate Organization

International Baccalaureate Organization, *IB Middle Years Programme Further guidance for MYP projects*, 2016, Geneva, Switzerland, International Baccalaureate Organization

Brand, W. 2017, *Visual Thinking*, Amsterdam, Netherlands, BIS Publishers

Hoang, P and Taylor, C. 2017, *Extended essay for the IB Diploma*, London, UK, Hodder Education

Kleon, A. 2014, *Show Your Work*, New York, USA, Workman Publishing Company, Inc.

Ritchhart, R, Church, M and Morrison K. 2011, *Making Thinking Visible*, San Francisco, USA, Jossey-Bass

Orders: please contact Bookpoint Ltd, 130 Park Drive, Milton Park, Abingdon, Oxon OX14 4SE.
Telephone: (44) 01235 827720. Fax: (44) 01235 400401. Email education@bookpoint.co.uk Lines are open from 9 a.m. to 5 p.m., Monday to Saturday, with a 24-hour message answering service. You can also order through our website: www.hoddereducation.com

ISBN: 9781510446595

First published in 2018 by
Hodder Education,
An Hachette UK Company
Carmelite House
50 Victoria Embankment
London EC4Y 0DZ

www.hoddereducation.com

Impression number 10 9 8 7 6 5 4 3 2

Year 2022 2021 2020 2019

Cover photo © sdecoret - stock.adobe.com

Illustrations by Aptara Inc.

Typeset in India by Aptara Inc.

Printed in Spain

A catalogue record for this title is available from the British Library.

FSC www.fsc.org
MIX
Paper from responsible sources
FSC™ C104740

Contents

Introduction

How to use this book

Welcome to the personal project for the IB MYP: Skills for Success.

This guide will help you prepare for your personal project in an efficient and logical way.

Each chapter of the book looks at a different aspect of the project in detail, while practice exercises are also included to help you check your understanding, and put the guidance into practice.

To ensure students demonstrate their best work in the personal project, this guide:

- includes an opening infographics spread in each chapter
- builds skills for success through a range of strategies and detailed expert advice, such as planning the best format for your report
- covers all the IB requirements with clear and concise explanations, such as the assessment criteria and rules on academic honesty
- demonstrates what is required to demonstrate your best work
- adds reference to the IB learner profile.

Key features of this guide include:

ATL skills

ATL skills covered are highlighted at the start of Chapters 2–9 and within each Activity. It is important to note that this is where you often have opportunities to demonstrate these skills, but they are not limited to these situations; any ATL skills can be demonstrated at any point.

LEARNER PROFILE ATTRIBUTES

Learner profile attributes are also highlighted at the start of Chapters 2–9.

EXPERT TIP

These tips appear throughout the book and provide guidance on steps you can take and key things you should consider in order to help you achieve your best.

ACTIVITY

Activities appear throughout the book, and provide you with the chance to put the skills and strategies into practice, to help you think about how to best approach your personal project.

Supervisor check-in

Chapters 3–7 end with a checklist for your next supervisor meeting.

CHAPTER SUMMARY KEY POINTS

At the end of Chapters 1, 3–7 and 10, key knowledge is distilled into a short checklist to help you review everything you have learnt over the previous pages.

About the authors

Laura England is a Language & Literature and Design teacher at Good Shepherd Lutheran College in Darwin, Australia and is also a member of the Building Quality Curriculum reviewer team. Previously she was the MYP Coordinator and MYP Projects Coordinator for five years and during this time also served the Good Shepherd community of learners as Head of Design and Head of Language Acquisition. Prior to teaching Laura worked in advertising and co-owned and operated a photography business.

Angela Stancar Johnson is Head of English at Southbank International School in London, where she was previously the MYP Projects Coordinator. She has taught MYP Language & Literature and DP English Literature and Language & Literature for the past nine years. Angela has in the past served as a moderator for the personal project and as an examiner for DP English and currently examines the MYP Interdisciplinary eAssessment. She also has experience in teaching high school journalism in the USA and has worked internationally in the scholastic publishing industry.

Understanding the

Vizualizing the project objectives

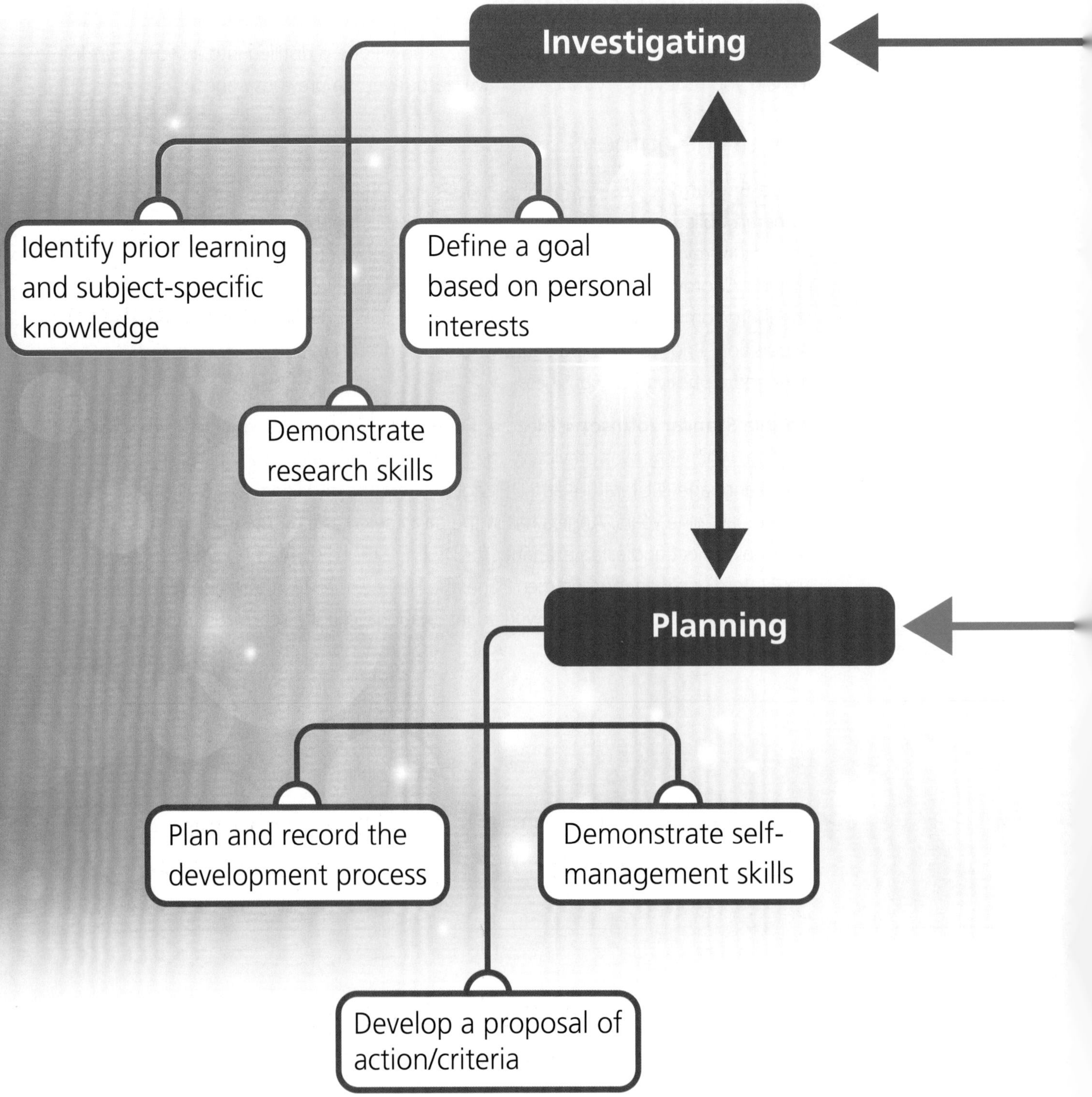
Investigating
Identify prior learning and subject-specific knowledge
Define a goal based on personal interests
Demonstrate research skills
Planning
Plan and record the development process
Demonstrate self-management skills
Develop a proposal of action/criteria

Personal Project objectives

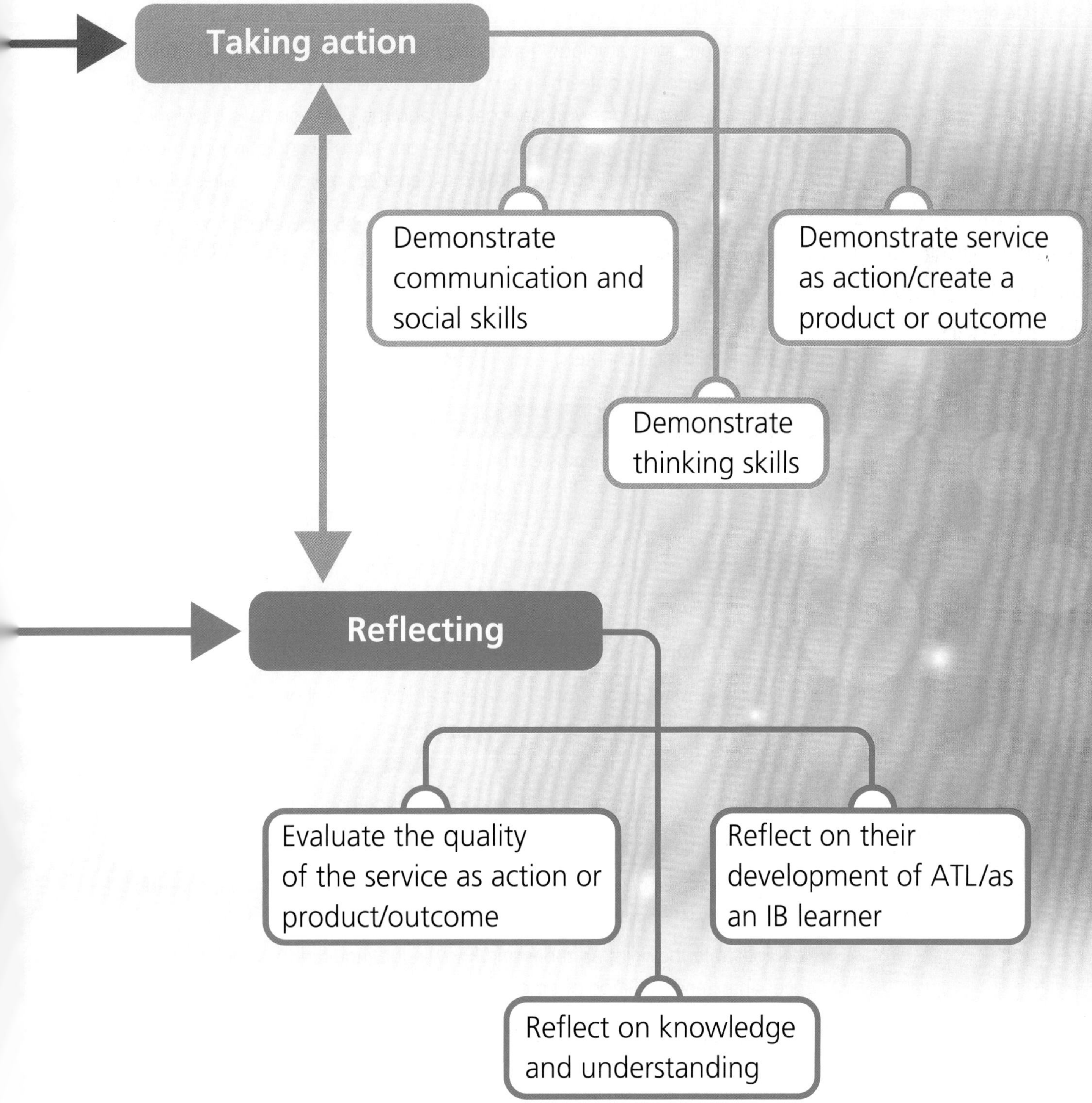
Taking action
Demonstrate communication and social skills
Demonstrate service as action/create a product or outcome
Demonstrate thinking skills
Reflecting
Evaluate the quality of the service as action or product/outcome
Reflect on their development of ATL/as an IB learner
Reflect on knowledge and understanding

CHAPTER 1

Understanding the Personal Project objectives

What is the Personal Project?

The personal project forms part of the core of the International Baccalaureate Middle Years Programme and is a significant milestone in your journey as an IB learner. It serves as both the culmination of your MYP studies and as a stepping stone towards future academic work, and the DP core. As part of the continuum, it is also a progression from the Community Project that you may have completed in MYP 3, and the PYP Exhibition.

EXPERT TIP

It is important to note that the personal project must not be linked to the curriculum or assessment of any of your subjects. However, the work you do in your subjects may support you in the development of your personal project.

The personal project is a unique opportunity to learn more about a topic that really interests you personally or learn a new skill (or develop an existing one) while also showcasing the knowledge you have gained and the skills you have developed throughout the MYP. If approached with the right attitude and mindset, the personal project can be one of the most rewarding experiences of your IB course of study.

The personal project is required of all students in MYP 5; however, in many schools you might begin the process in MYP 4.

The personal project consists of three parts: the process journal, the product or outcome, and the report. How to approach each of these parts will be covered in detail in the following chapters.

EXPERT TIP

Many schools host a formal personal project Exhibition which gives you the opportunity to showcase and celebrate your hard work with an audience of fellow students, teachers, parents, and community members. If this is part of your school's tradition, you will receive information about what and how to present from your supervisor, Personal Project Coordinator and/or MYP Coordinator.

Personal Project aims

Aims are general statements which relate to an overall goal or intended outcome. The personal project aims state what you may expect to experience and learn through the process of inquiry.

The aims of the MYP projects are to encourage and enable students to:

- participate in a sustained, self-directed inquiry within a global context
- generate creative new insights and develop deeper understandings through in-depth investigation
- demonstrate the skills, attitudes and knowledge required to complete a project over an extended period of time
- communicate effectively in a variety of situations
- demonstrate responsible action through, or as a result of, learning
- appreciate the process of learning and take pride in their accomplishments.

Personal Project objectives

Objectives are specific steps along the journey towards the end goal. The personal project objectives define what you will be able to accomplish as a result of your study.

There are four main objectives, each of which align with the assessment criteria:

- Investigating
- Planning
- Taking action
- Reflecting.

Each objective is broken down further into three separate strands which relate to the overall objective.

Understanding the assessment criteria

As mentioned in the last section, the assessment criteria directly align with the project objectives. Each criterion has 8 levels of achievement. It is worth noting that a majority of the levels are awarded based on the *process*; only Criterion C directly assesses the *product*. The tables below are taken from the personal project assessment criteria for Year 5.

Criterion A	
Investigating (8 levels) This is the starting point of your project. You start by investigating, but you may end up following the inquiry cycle (inquiry, action, reflection) more than once in order to strengthen, extend or refine your inquiry. Criterion A assesses your ability to: i define a clear goal and a global context for the project, based on personal interests ii identify prior learning and subject-specific knowledge relevant to the project iii demonstrate research skills.	
Achievement level	**Level descriptor**
0	The student **does not** achieve a standard described by any of the descriptors below.
1–2	The student: i **states** a goal and context for the project, based on personal interests, but this may be **limited** in depth or accessibility ii identifies prior learning and subject-specific knowledge, **but** this may be **limited** in occurrence or relevance iii demonstrates **limited** research skills.
3–4	The student: i **outlines** a **basic and appropriate** goal and a global context for the project, based on personal interests ii identifies **basic** prior learning and subject-specific knowledge **relevant** to **some** areas of the project iii demonstrates **adequate** research skills.
5–6	The student: i **develops** a **clear and challenging** goal and a global context for the project, based on personal interests ii identifies prior learning and subject-specific knowledge **generally relevant** to the project iii demonstrates **substantial** research skills.

7–8	The student: i **develops** a **clear and highly challenging** goal and a global context for the project, based on personal interests ii identifies prior learning and subject-specific knowledge that is **consistently highly relevant** to the project iii demonstrates **excellent** research skills.

Criterion B

Planning (8 levels)

This includes all the work you will do to plan and organize your project towards a product/outcome.

Criterion B assesses your ability to:

i develop criteria for the product/outcome
ii plan and record the development process of the project
iii demonstrate self-management skills.

Achievement level	Level descriptor
0	The student **does not** achieve a standard described by any of the descriptors below.
1–2	The student: i develops **limited** criteria for the product/outcome ii presents a **limited or partial** plan and record of the development process of the project iii demonstrates **limited** self-management skills.
3–4	The student: i develops **adequate** criteria for the product/outcome ii presents an **adequate** plan and record of the development process of the project iii demonstrates **adequate** self-management skills.
5–6	The student: i develops **substantial and appropriate** criteria for the product/outcome ii presents a **substantial** plan and record of the development process of the project iii demonstrates **substantial** self-management skills.
7–8	The student: i develops **rigorous** criteria for the product/outcome ii presents a **detailed and accurate** plan and record of the development process of the project iii demonstrates **excellent** self-management skills.

Criterion C	
Taking action (8 levels) This is the main "doing" part of your project – the action part of the inquiry cycle – where the product/outcome is developed and completed. Criterion C assesses your ability to: i create a product/outcome in response to the goal, global context and criteria ii demonstrate thinking skills iii demonstrate communication and social skills.	
Achievement level	**Level descriptor**
0	The student **does not** achieve a standard described by any of the descriptors below.
1–2	The student: i creates a **limited** product/outcome in response to the goal, global context and criteria ii demonstrates **limited** thinking skills iii demonstrates **limited** communication and social skills.
3–4	The student: i creates a **basic** product/outcome in response to the goal, global context and criteria ii demonstrates **adequate** thinking skills iii demonstrates **adequate** communication and social skills.
5–6	The student: i creates a **substantial** product/outcome in response to the goal, global context and criteria ii demonstrates **substantial** thinking skills iii demonstrates **substantial** communication and social skills.
7–8	The student: i creates an **excellent** product/outcome in response to the goal, global context and criteria ii demonstrates **excellent** thinking skills iii demonstrates **excellent** communication and social skills.

Criterion D	
Reflecting (8 levels) This is the point when you look back over the project and evaluate your development. You may have reflected during the process of the project and you can refer to this here too. Criterion D assesses your ability to: i evaluate the quality of the product/success of the outcome against your criteria ii reflect on how completing the project has extended your knowledge and understanding of the topic and the global context iii reflect on your development as an IB learner through the project.	
Achievement level	**Level descriptor**
0	The student **does not** achieve a standard described by any of the descriptors below.
1–2	The student: i presents a **limited** evaluation of the quality of the product/success of the outcome against his or her criteria ii presents **limited** reflection on how completing the project has extended his or her knowledge and understanding of the topic and the global context iii presents **limited** reflection on his or her development as an IB learner through the project.
3–4	The student: i presents a **basic** evaluation of the quality of the product/success of the outcome against his or her criteria ii presents **adequate** reflection on how completing the project has extended his or her knowledge and understanding of the topic and the global context iii presents **adequate** reflection on his or her development as an IB learner through the project.
5–6	The student: i presents a **substantial** evaluation of the quality of the product/success of the outcome against his or her criteria ii presents **substantial** reflection on how completing the project has extended his or her knowledge and understanding of the topic and the global context iii presents **substantial** reflection on his or her development as an IB learner through the project.
7–8	The student: i presents an **excellent** evaluation of the quality of the product/success of the outcome against his or her criteria ii presents **excellent** reflection on how completing the project has extended his or her knowledge and understanding of the topic and the global context iii presents **excellent** reflection on his or her development as an IB learner through the project.

CHAPTER SUMMARY KEY POINTS

- The personal project is the culminating project of the IB Middle Years Programme. It is a progression from the PYP Exhibition and MYP Community Project, and a stepping stone towards the outcomes of the DP core.
- All students in MYP 5 are required to complete a personal project.
- The personal project must not be linked to any subject-specific curriculum or assessment.
- The personal project consists of three parts: the process journal, the product or outcome and the report.
- You will be assessed on four criteria, each with 8 levels of achievement (like your other MYP subjects).
- The criteria you will be assessed on are:
  - Investigating
  - Planning
  - Taking action
  - Reflecting.
- Only Criterion C directly assesses the product or outcome.

The Process

The process journal is used throughout the project to document its development. It is an evolving record of intents, processes, and accomplishments.

The process journal is a place to record initial thoughts and developments, brainstorming, possible lines of inquiry and further questions raised.

The process journal is a record of reflections and formative feedback received.

The process journal is a place for recording interactions with sources, for example teachers, supervisors and external contributors.

It is a place to record selected, annotated and/or edited research and to maintain a bibliography.

Journal

The process journal is a place for evaluation of work to be completed.

It is a place for reflecting on learning.

It should be devised by you, the student, in a format that suits your needs.

The process journal is a place for storing useful information, for example quotations, pictures, ideas and photographs.

The process journal is a means of exploring ideas and solutions.

CHAPTER 2

The Process Journal

ATL skills

- Reflection skills
- Organizational skills

LEARNER PROFILE ATTRIBUTES

Thinkers	Communicators	Reflective

Recording the development process of your project

The "process journal" is a generic term used to refer to your self-maintained record of progress that you make throughout your personal project journey. Before you begin your personal project journey, you will need to organize a process journal.

The format of the process journal is completely up to you. Examples of what you may want to use are a notebook, online blog, iBook, Word document, OneNote book, visual art diary or a combination of the ideas here – it is entirely up to you. You simply must ensure that you backup your process journal continuously – this is an important responsibility.

Your process journal is a place where you record your thoughts, ideas, problem solving, reflections, responses to questions, inquiry questions, research, images, inspirations, photos/videos of progress, interviews ... basically every aspect of your personal project! The process journal is also where you will demonstrate being a principled learner through recording academic honesty.

Your peers, family, friends, teachers, supervisor or any other interested person should be able to have a very clear understanding of your personal project journey simply by reading your process journal. The four objectives of the personal project – investigating, planning, taking action and reflecting – should be evident in your process journal. The process journal is what makes your personal project journey visible.

To further clarify just what the process journal is the IBO have provided you with an outline of what the process journal is and what it is not.

The process journal is:	The process journal is not:
• used throughout the project to document its development • an evolving record of intents, processes, accomplishments • a place to record initial thoughts and developments, brainstorming, possible lines of inquiry and further questions raised • a place for recording interactions with sources, for example teachers, supervisors, external contributors • a place to record selected, annotated and/or edited research and to maintain a bibliography • a place for storing useful information, for example quotations, pictures, ideas, photographs • a means of exploring ideas and solutions • a place for evaluation work completed • a place for reflecting on learning • devised by you, the student, in a format that suits your needs • a record of reflections and formative feedback received.	• used on a daily basis (unless this is useful for your project) • written up after the process has been completed • additional work on top of the project; it is part of the project and supports the project • a diary with detailed writing about what was done • a static document with only one format.

The personal project is a creative endeavour. You are making something truly unique and personal. This is worth sharing. In your process journal, show your work. It deserves to be seen.

Examples of process journals

To support you in understanding the role and purpose of the personal project process journal, below is a series of extracts that show each of the personal project objectives evident in a variety of formats.

Objective A: Investigating

This student has documented their personal project goal in a visual art diary, a format chosen to complement the artistic nature of their personal project topic and goal.

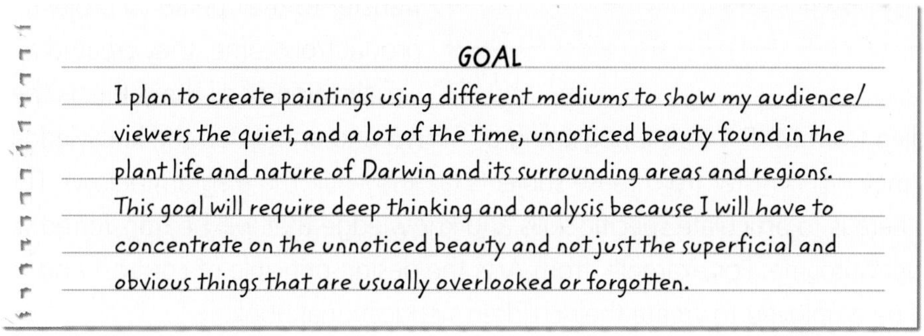
GOAL
I plan to create paintings using different mediums to show my audience/ viewers the quiet, and a lot of the time, unnoticed beauty found in the plant life and nature of Darwin and its surrounding areas and regions. This goal will require deep thinking and analysis because I will have to concentrate on the unnoticed beauty and not just the superficial and obvious things that are usually overlooked or forgotten.

Using a global context exploration lens, this student has taken the time to explore all the possibilities of their personal project topic through the lens of each of the global contexts.

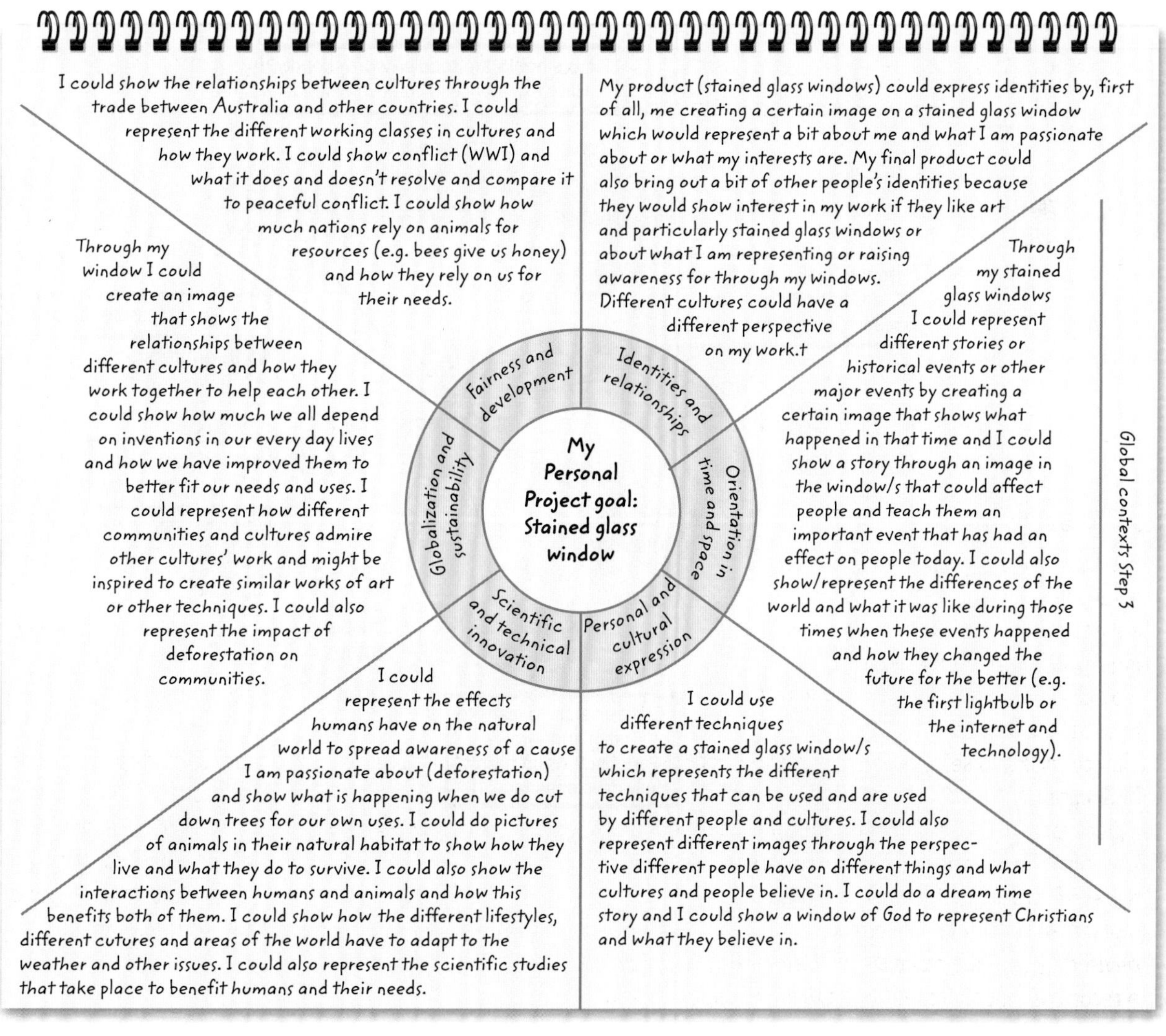
My Personal Project goal: Stained glass window
Fairness and development
Identities and relationships
Orientation in time and space
Personal and cultural expression
Scientific and technical innovation
Globalization and sustainability
I could show the relationships between cultures through the trade between Australia and other countries. I could represent the different working classes in cultures and how they work. I could show conflict (WWI) and what it does and doesn't resolve and compare it to peaceful conflict. I could show how much nations rely on animals for resources (e.g. bees give us honey) and how they rely on us for their needs.
My product (stained glass windows) could express identities by, first of all, me creating a certain image on a stained glass window which would represent a bit about me and what I am passionate about or what my interests are. My final product could also bring out a bit of other people's identities because they would show interest in my work if they like art and particularly stained glass windows or about what I am representing or raising awareness for through my windows. Different cultures could have a different perspective on my work.t
Through my stained glass windows I could represent different stories or historical events or other major events by creating a certain image that shows what happened in that time and I could show a story through an image in the window/s that could affect people and teach them an important event that has had an effect on people today. I could also show/represent the differences of the world and what it was like during those times when these events happened and how they changed the future for the better (e.g. the first lightbulb or the internet and technology).
I could use different techniques to create a stained glass window/s which represents the different techniques that can be used and are used by different people and cultures. I could also represent different images through the perspective different people have on different things and what cultures and people believe in. I could do a dream time story and I could show a window of God to represent Christians and what they believe in.
I could represent the effects humans have on the natural world to spread awareness of a cause I am passionate about (deforestation) and show what is happening when we do cut down trees for our own uses. I could do pictures of animals in their natural habitat to show how they live and what they do to survive. I could also show the interactions between humans and animals and how this benefits both of them. I could show how the different lifestyles, different cutures and areas of the world have to adapt to the weather and other issues. I could also represent the scientific studies that take place to benefit humans and their needs.
Through my window I could create an image that shows the relationships between different cultures and how they work together to help each other. I could show how much we all depend on inventions in our every day lives and how we have improved them to better fit our needs and uses. I could represent how different communities and cultures admire other cultures' work and might be inspired to create similar works of art or other techniques. I could also represent the impact of deforestation on communities.
Global contexts Step 3

> **Prior learning 15/5/15**
> What do you already know about your product/outcome?
> I have a lot of knowledge of music, both outside school and inside, with knowing how to play saxophone really well & piano, drums and flute to a basic standard key in this.
> I also know about timing and a little bit about metal fabrication from my father who has done some at house on the trailer (camping) and boat.
> For the past 5 years I have played the sax.
> Through this I have also learnt timing, though not significant my understanding of the steel fabrication comes from my father.
> This is useful because it means that the second part of my outcome, learning to play it, will be easier as well as the timing, though it will still be incredibly difficult. Though not very useful, my basic knowledge of steel and metal work may increase my confidence.

To help this personal project student break down their prior learning they have reflected on the knowledge and skills they already have of musicianship, their level of skill and knowledge and what they will find challenging to acquire through the process of creating their product/outcome (see extract to the left).

To show all the subject-specific knowledge that this student would transfer to their personal project product/outcome, they created a visualization of all the subjects they have studied from MYP 1 to the beginning of MYP 5 and annotated the knowledge and skills they will transfer from these subjects (as shown in the diagram below). The next step here is to articulate specific skills and knowledge that will be transferred to the product/outcome. For example, from Arts the design principle of contrast and space will be employed to create their children's educational book.

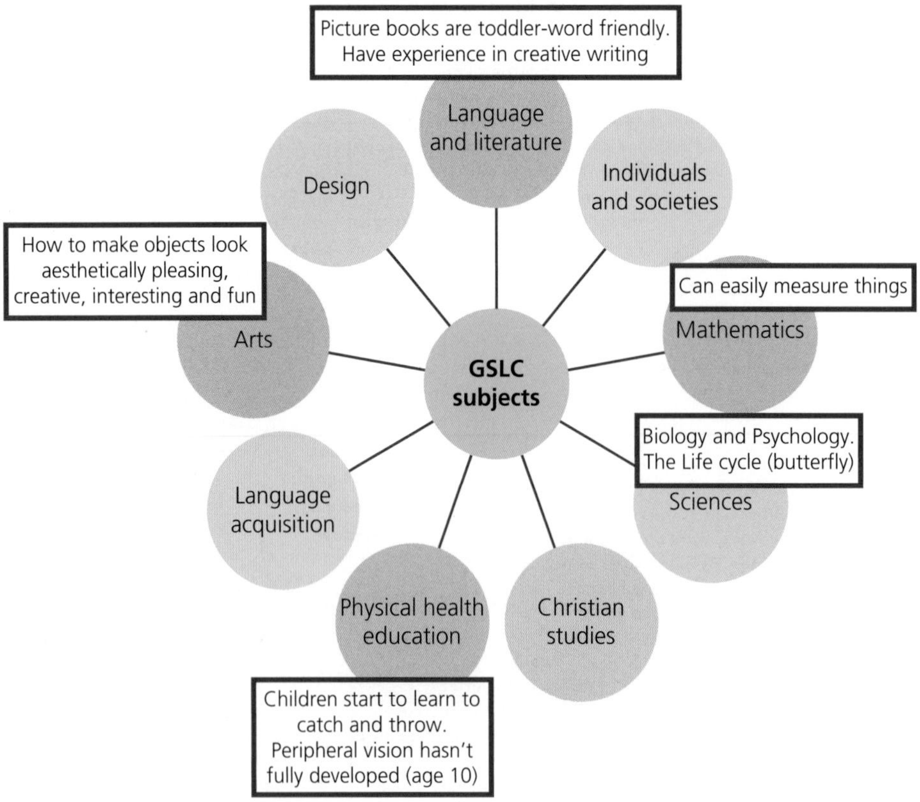
Picture books are toddler-word friendly. Have experience in creative writing
Language and literature
Design
Individuals and societies
How to make objects look aesthetically pleasing, creative, interesting and fun
Arts
Can easily measure things
Mathematics
GSLC subjects
Biology and Psychology. The Life cycle (butterfly)
Sciences
Language acquisition
Physical health education
Christian studies
Children start to learn to catch and throw. Peripheral vision hasn't fully developed (age 10)

To support their research process into how to create a Hang (a musical instrument) this student began by listing a series of research questions and identifying whether they will need to be primary or secondary sources. On the corresponding page of their process journal they have added greater detail to the specifics of what they will need to research.

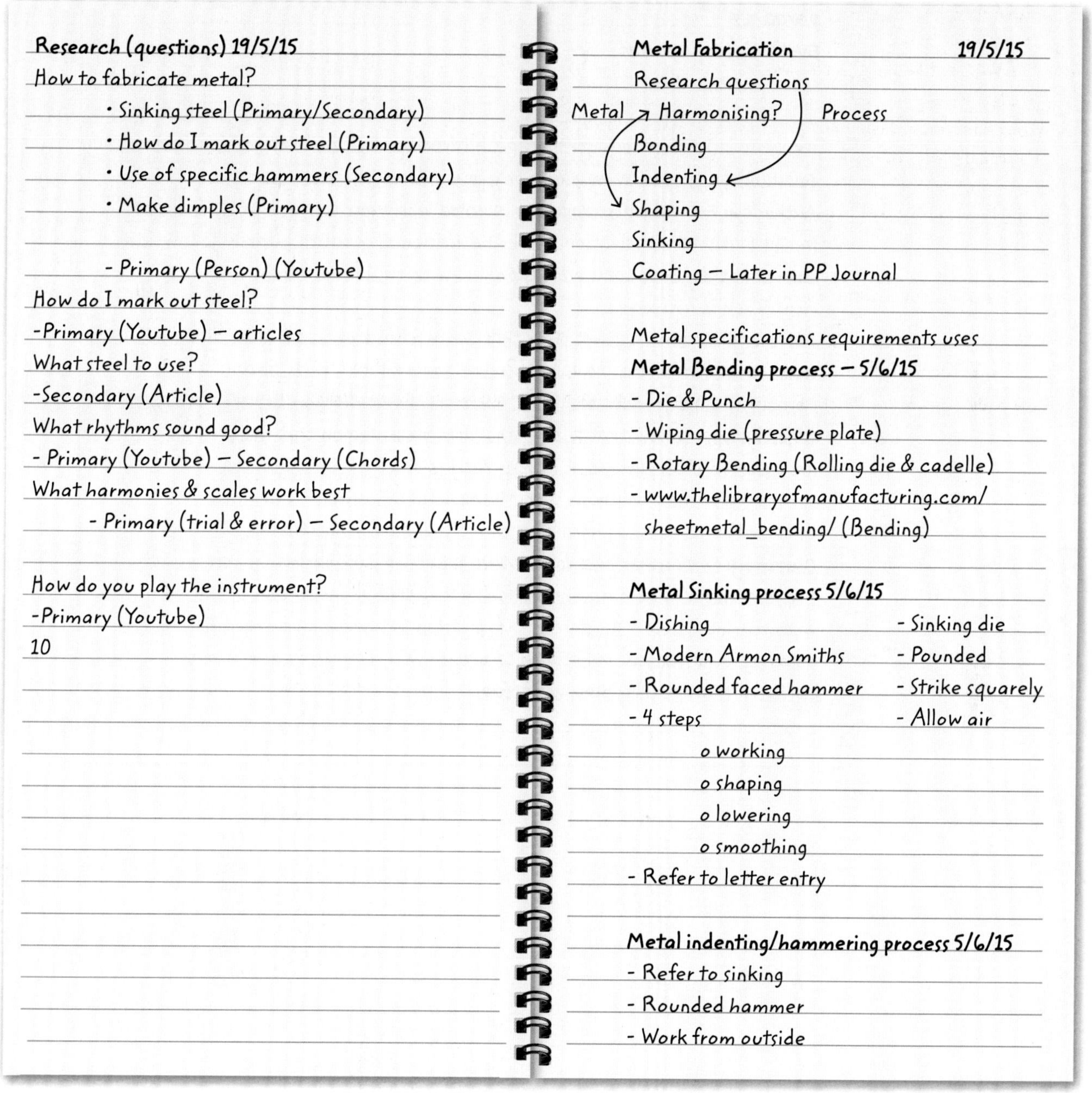

Research (questions) 19/5/15

How to fabricate metal?

- Sinking steel (Primary/Secondary)
- How do I mark out steel (Primary)
- Use of specific hammers (Secondary)
- Make dimples (Primary)

- Primary (Person) (Youtube)

How do I mark out steel?

-Primary (Youtube) – articles

What steel to use?

-Secondary (Article)

What rhythms sound good?

- Primary (Youtube) – Secondary (Chords)

What harmonies & scales work best

- Primary (trial & error) – Secondary (Article)

How do you play the instrument?

-Primary (Youtube)

10

Metal Fabrication 19/5/15

Research questions

Metal → Harmonising? Process

Bonding

Indenting

Shaping

Sinking

Coating – Later in PP Journal

Metal specifications requirements uses

Metal Bending process – 5/6/15

- Die & Punch
- Wiping die (pressure plate)
- Rotary Bending (Rolling die & cadelle)
- www.thelibraryofmanufacturing.com/sheetmetal_bending/ (Bending)

Metal Sinking process 5/6/15

- Dishing
- Modern Armon Smiths
- Rounded faced hammer
- 4 steps
  - o working
  - o shaping
  - o lowering
  - o smoothing
- Refer to letter entry

- Sinking die
- Pounded
- Strike squarely
- Allow air

Metal indenting/hammering process 5/6/15

- Refer to sinking
- Rounded hammer
- Work from outside

To ensure their sources are accurate and reliable, this student has documented their analysis of sources in their process journal and clearly labelled the authority, accuracy, objectivity and currency of the source. To ensure the correct information is accessible to add to their bibliography they have included the URL at the top of the page.

26/02/17

Evaluation of Sources

Secondary

Primary

Anon, (n.d.) "Good Toys for Young Children by Age and Stage." [online] Available at: https://www.naeyc.org/toys [Accessed = 22/02/17]

Authority: From the direct page it is noted who wrote it. The NAEYC stands for The National Association for the Education of Young Children so it would seem that they have some professional say on the information. How much is unknown.

Accuracy: Again I cannot prove that the information is accurate due to the unknown writer, however there are some related links and Consumer Safety Websites listed. Therefore the website isn't totally dodgy!

Objectivity: I believe that a lot of the facts presented on this website are based on observations. It is very easy to observe a child, compare to others and see a common theme/behaviour. Of course it may well be biased as no other sources have been cited, author mentioned.

Currency: The author has not provided a date of publication, however I believe that it is no older than 2005; date listed at the bottom of the website (not article). The date of information is always important for accurate information. What a child played with 100 years ago is very different to what they play with today.

Objective B: Planning

This student has listed the specifications required for their personal project product/outcome to be effective.

Aesthetics	The appearance of my booklet should be appealing to majority of ages that are girls. The layout must be logical and easy to follow. The colours and fonts chosen also need to be easy to read and not harsh on the eye.
Cost	The cost of the project shouldn't exceed $500. The majority of money will be spent on food to create and trial the recipes, however all the food will be eaten so it is not being wasted. My mum said she can print the booklet at work so I will be saving on ink.
Customer	The booklet is targeted towards 14-18 year old girls who play netball. They are interested in eating healthy and improving their play. It is also for vegetarians, whether netballer or not.
Resources	There are no limited resources for me to make my booklet. I already own a tablet/laptop with Word on it and my mother and supervisor have both offered to print the final copy.
Environment consideration	As my booklet will use a fair bit of paper to print I will be limiting my max amount of copies to 15 only if needed. This way I ensure I am not using the earth's resources unthoughtfully.
Function	The purpose of my project is to create a booklet that contains information on nutrition for vegetarians playing netball and recipes. I want it to be something people can look at when they aren't sure what to eat.
Size	The size of the booklet will be minimal as it won't have over 50 pages in it.

This student has transferred their specifications and created criteria for success that they have used to self-assess and evaluate the quality of their product/outcome, in the table below.

Water lily painting

	Specification 1: identifiable	Specification 2: creative-thinking	Specification 3: art techniques	Specification 4: research	Specification 5: effort	Specification 6: detail
Simply stunning (7-8)	As soon as people see the piece it's immediately recognisable as based on Darwin	The piece explicitly shows that there was a lot of creative-thinking	Piece shows four effective art techniques	There is abundant proof that research has been done	Proof that a great deal of effort has been used	Great detail has been put into it
Eye-catching beautiful (5-6)	With little explanation, the piece is recognisable as based on Darwin	There is considerable proof that there was creative-thinking	The piece shows three effective art techniques	There is considerable proof that research has been done	Proof that a substantial amount of effort has been used	Substantial amount of detail has been put into it
Aesthetically pleasing (3-4)	Piece needs to be explained to be recognisable as based on Darwin	There was satisfactory proof that there was creative-thinking	The piece shows at least two effective art techniques	There is adequate proof that research has been done	There is satisfactory proof of effort being used	Adequate amount of detail has been put into it
Plain, boring scribbles (1-2)	Unrecognisable as based on Darwin even with explanation given	There was little to no proof that there was creative-thinking	The piece shows one effective art technique	There is little to no proof that research has been done	There is little to no proof of effort being used	Little to no detail has been put into it

To plan ahead and ensure they were organized and had sufficient time to achieve their personal project goal, this student created a timeline in their process journal with colour-coded keys to help them organize their project.

The remainder of the timeline is continued throughout their process journal all the way to the due date.

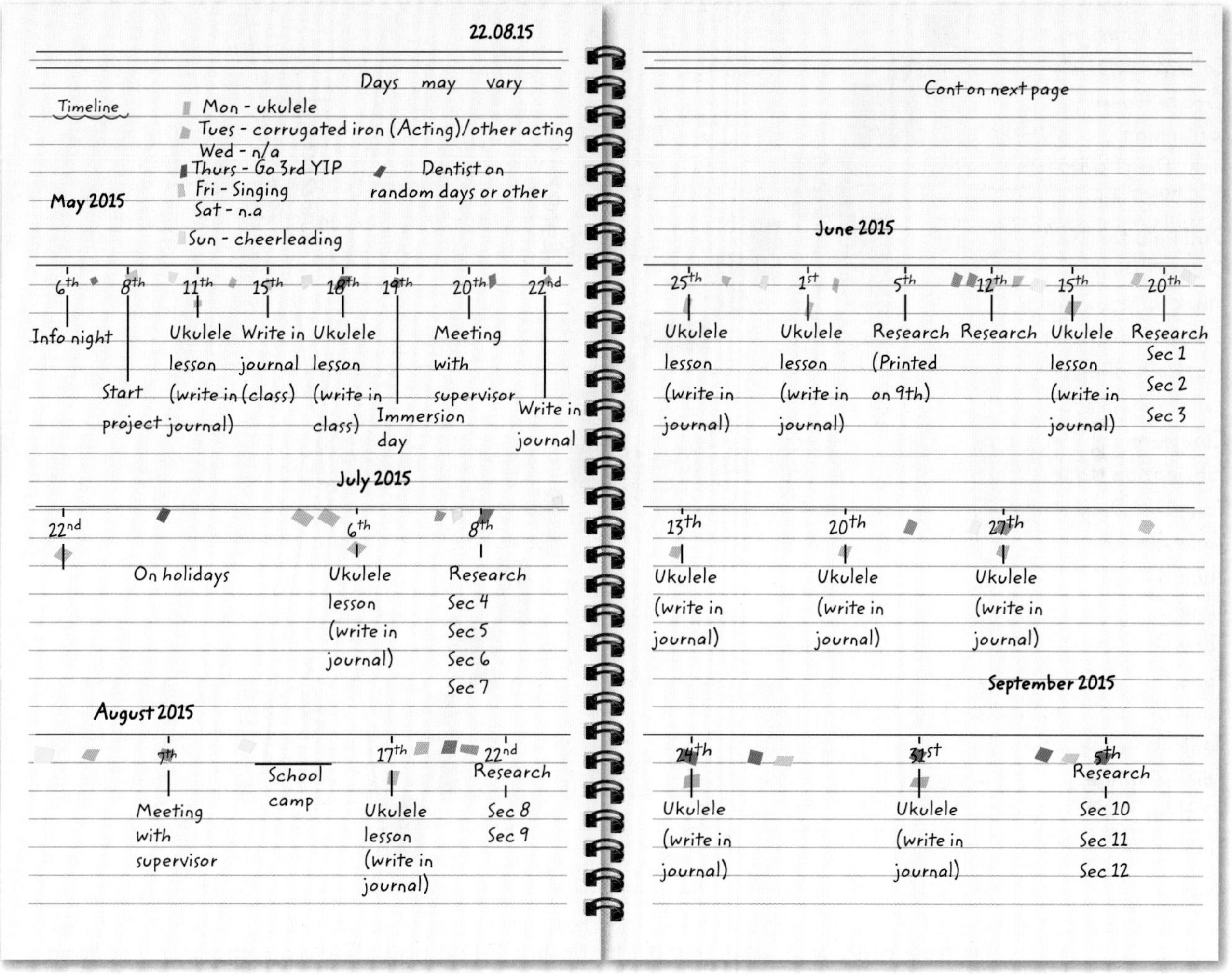
22.08.15
Days may vary
Timeline
Mon - ukulele
Tues - corrugated iron (Acting)/other acting
Wed - n/a
Thurs - Go 3rd YIP
Dentist on random days or other
Fri - Singing
Sat - n.a
Sun - cheerleading
May 2015
6th 8th 11th 15th 18th 19th 20th 22nd
Info night
Start project journal)
Ukulele lesson (write in
Write in journal (class)
Ukulele lesson (write in class)
Immersion day
Meeting with supervisor
Write in journal
July 2015
22nd
On holidays
6th
Ukulele lesson (write in journal)
8th
Research Sec 4 Sec 5 Sec 6 Sec 7
August 2015
7th
Meeting with supervisor
School camp
17th
Ukulele lesson (write in journal)
22nd
Research Sec 8 Sec 9
Cont on next page
June 2015
25th
Ukulele lesson (write in journal)
1st
Ukulele lesson (write in journal)
5th
Research (Printed on 9th)
12th
Research
15th
Ukulele lesson (write in journal)
20th
Research Sec 1 Sec 2 Sec 3
13th
Ukulele (write in journal)
20th
Ukulele (write in journal)
27th
Ukulele (write in journal)
September 2015
24th
Ukulele (write in journal)
31st
Ukulele (write in journal)
5th
Research Sec 10 Sec 11 Sec 12

This student has created a Gantt chart to plan for the completion of the creation of their product/outcome and have ensured they factored in rest time in a family holiday. Down the left-hand side they have broken each aspect of taking action into steps and have planned the time frame for completing these in the corresponding chart.

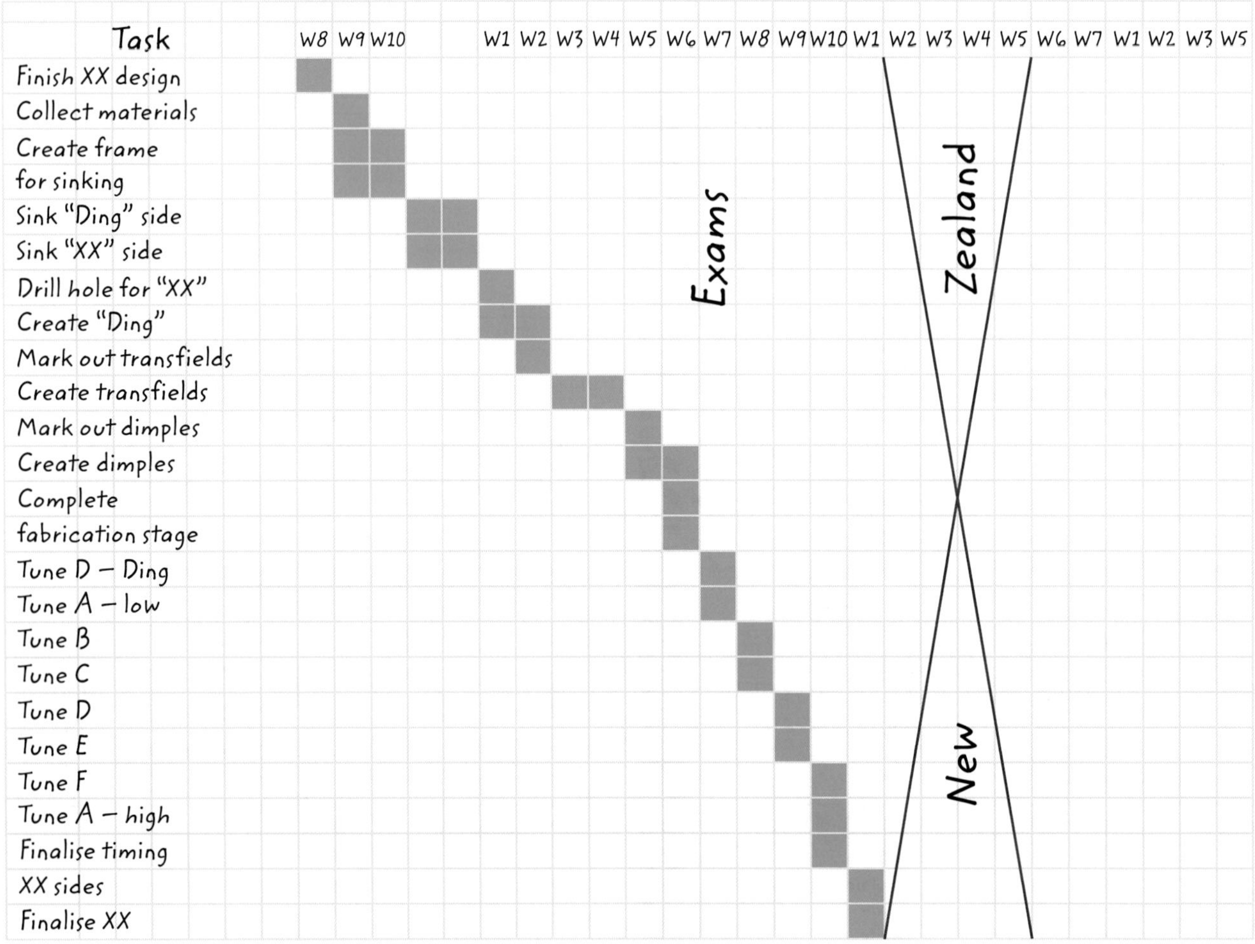
Task
W8 W9 W10
W1 W2 W3 W4 W5 W6 W7 W8 W9 W10 W1 W2 W3 W4 W5 W6 W7 W1 W2 W3 W5
Finish XX design
Collect materials
Create frame for sinking
Sink "Ding" side
Sink "XX" side
Drill hole for "XX"
Create "Ding"
Mark out transfields
Create transfields
Mark out dimples
Create dimples
Complete fabrication stage
Tune D – Ding
Tune A – low
Tune B
Tune C
Tune D
Tune E
Tune F
Tune A – high
Finalise timing
XX sides
Finalise XX
Exams
New Zealand

In their process journal, this student reflected on how they were struggling to keep on track and complete their personal project in the time frames they had assigned to themselves, so they set personal goals and adjusted their plans to ensure they were able to make their personal project a priority.

Demonstrate self-management skills

When I started the project, I was determined and enthused about the task. I had spent a lot of time getting inspiration from different images and I wanted to find a photo nearly exactly to what I wanted to achieve. However, as the weeks went on I found myself less interested in the project and my focus was spent in other aspects of my life. To overcome this, I told myself that I couldn't do my learner's permit test until I finished my project. This gave me the will to finish my project as getting my 'L's was important to me.

Objective C: Taking action

Throughout the process of creating their personal project product/outcome, this student documented the process and recorded their reflections. Note how they have added the dates as further evidence of managing their time and keeping within the time frames allotted to them.

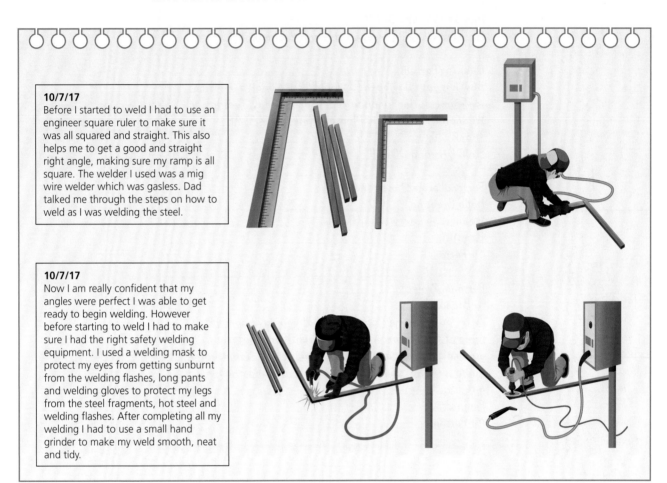

10/7/17
Before I started to weld I had to use an engineer square ruler to make sure it was all squared and straight. This also helps me to get a good and straight right angle, making sure my ramp is all square. The welder I used was a mig wire welder which was gasless. Dad talked me through the steps on how to weld as I was welding the steel.

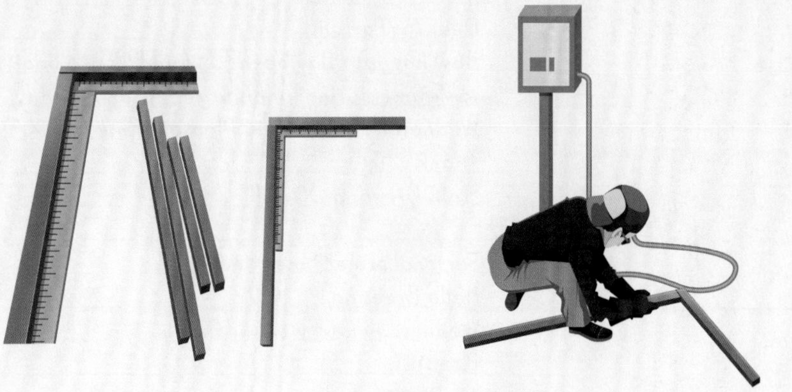

10/7/17
Now I am really confident that my angles were perfect I was able to get ready to begin welding. However before starting to weld I had to make sure I had the right safety welding equipment. I used a welding mask to protect my eyes from getting sunburnt from the welding flashes, long pants and welding gloves to protect my legs from the steel fragments, hot steel and welding flashes. After completing all my welding I had to use a small hand grinder to make my weld smooth, neat and tidy.

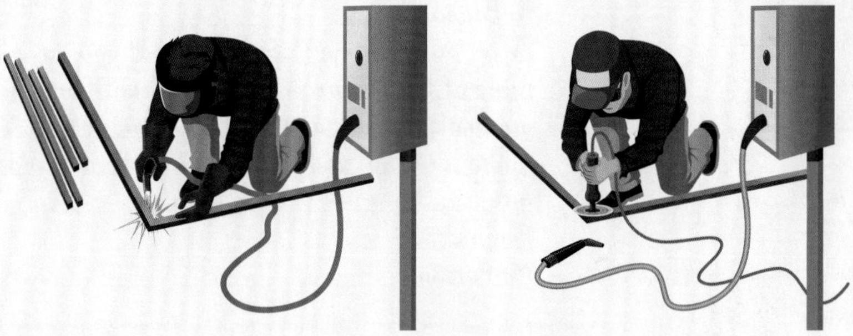

In order to demonstrate thinking skills, this student chose to reflect in their process journal how they have practised creative-thinking skills.

How have you developed flexible thinking strategies by playing devil's advocate surrounding the ethical impact of your product?
Since we live in a time of gender discrimination and identity I have tried my best to keep my product gender neutral. I have also thought of the environmental impact of my product. The materials used are not environmentally friendly so therefore I have re-used a majority of them throughout my product, limiting waste.

As a means of providing evidence of communication with their supervisor, this student took screenshots of their email communication and added this to their process journal.

Meeting emails
May 19 2015 at 2:06PM,
Breeana O'Neill (breeana.student@school.net) wrote:

Dear Mr Parsons,
How has your day been? I would like to book a meeting sometime during lunch or recess on Monday, Tuesday or Wednesday next week. Please let me know ASAP
Thank you,
From Breeana O'Neill

Personal project meeting
Hello Breeana,
Wednesday next week is fine.
Regards,
Mr Parsons

Personal Project
Hi Breeana,
After our meeting I could see that you have completed some of the research including identifying materials, guiding questions and that you started well. You need to make sure that you order your materials and choose a fabric.
Regards,
Mr Parsons

You can also include in your process journal examples of surveys and notes from discussions with mentors and experts that you have communicated with.

Objective D: Reflecting

In their process journal, this student has self-assessed the quality of their personal project product/outcome using the criteria for success they have developed during planning. They have then explained their decisions accompanied with examples.

	Specification 1: 8	Specification 2: 4	Specification 3: 6
7-8 Excellent	The product is extremely colourful, quite overwhelming and is very detailed	There are more than 10 activities with different functions and purpose. The product contains over 5 materials.	The product cost less than $50 to make.
5-6 Substantial	The product is quite colourful and has many activities.	There are 10 activities, some with a purpose. The product contains 5 different materials.	The product cost up to $100 dollars to make
3-4 Adequate	The product is bland and underwhelming. It is not aesthetically pleasing.	There are between 5-10 activities which contain 3 different materials.	The product cost less than $150 to make.
1-2 Limited	The product is not eye-catching, is very boring and quite underwhelming.	There are less than 5 activities using less than 3 materials.	The product cost up to $200 or more to make
0 No evidence			

Reflecting

Present an excellent evaluation of the quality of the product/outcome against your criteria

Specification 1: 8/8
I agree with the criteria in that my product is very colourful and quite overwhelming for the eye. Therefore, this ensures that when the product is used a child's eyes are being stimulated, making them want to explore the reasons and uses of each page/activity.

Specification 2: 4/8
At the time when I created the criteria for success I had it in mind that I would have an activity on each side of the page, therefore doubling the amount of activities. If this were the case I would easily have had 10 activities, but as I was creating the product, thinking of pages with appropriate learning purposes became very difficult. However, I am very happy with my purpose-filled 7 activities, and with tweaking to this specification I believe that this criteria could earn at least a 6.
The only reason I had to give this specification a 4 and not higher was because of the number of activities I have, 7 (between 5 and 10). Where it could have gone higher is the second part of the specification which states, "contain three different materials." Throughout my product I have used between 10-20 materials, more than required to score an 8.

Specification 3: 6/8
Finishing the product, I have spent $70.94. Approximately 95% of the materials I used within my product were bought from a store, for the one purpose – to create my product.
The reason I gave this specification a 6 and not a 7 was because it did cost over my goal of $50, but wasn't half way between $50-$100 ($75). Had it been over $75 I would have given this specification a 5 as part of this goal was to spend as little as possible.

This student has demonstrated depth of thinking through reflecting on their newly developed understanding of the global context they have chosen.

Understanding the Global Context – I believe I have a better understanding of the global context "Identities and Relationships" after looking into the true identity of the chosen Greek gods and monsters. After researching how they were mistreated/misjudged I was able to gain a better understanding of them. Even though they were Gods and immortal monsters they still experienced human-like emotions such as sorrow, grief, heart ache, etc. What does it mean to be human? I can answer that question now after completing my personal project. Being human means you feel emotion, your heart and brain make you feel and react to certain emotions because they may affect you physically, spiritually or mentally. The reaction may be to actions, words or thoughts but they still cause emotions to be felt or displayed. What it means to be human? You are always destined to care.

In their process journal, this student has reflected on each of the IB learner profile attributes and explained how they have developed as an IB learner, using examples from their personal project journey.

Communicators:
Throughout the personal project every student is reminded of the importance of your process journal. For me, the process journal is the perfect opportunity to see my thoughts reflected on a page and easy for others to use and understand. Because of this I made sure that I frequently logged my ideas and thoughts so that I can look back on them for later times (creating my product). This is how I have developed as a communicator.

Having the knowledge and answer of the cure for cancer or a world without war is a great accomplishment. However, this information is useless to everyone unless the holder of this information is able to communicate it to others. Therefore learning how to communicate to others is a very important skill for younger people, like myself, and is something that is encouraged greatly during the first few years of schooling.

By communicating my ideas to others I have been able to receive feedback and helpful ideas. Due to this I then use those ideas for my product. Being a communicator helps me be a more compassionate learner as I am able to consider other people's input.

I will continue to communicate my thoughts and ideas as the next few years will be all about what I want to get out of my life, future and career. If people don't know what I want then I am not going to be able to achieve my goals.

Principled:
While planning for my product I thought a lot about how others may see it, based on the times that we live in; gender equality, sexual orientation, etc. I have then assessed how I can make these issues accepted within my product and this is how I have developed my principled characteristics.

One characteristic within being principled, that stands out for me, is: you act with a strong sense of fairness. Within today's society if you outcast someone by race, gender, religion, whatever it may be, the world will never be a peaceful place because there will always be a reason to disagree with something. So as a young person I believe that it is so important to be fair to others, yes you can have opinions but not against another human's life.
Developing as a principled person has made me a compassionate learner. Through my research I have had to understand other's situations and society's view and expectations on others.

As you can see from these examples from past personal project students, your process journal is where you document the journey of your personal project. It is a good idea to highlight the objectives in your process journal so at the end of your personal project when you are developing your report, you can easily access information that can support your report and also be added to your appendix.

Selecting process journal extracts

When developing your personal project report, you should carefully select evidence from your process journal to demonstrate the development of all criteria – investigating, planning, taking action and reflecting. These extracts are submitted as appendices of the report.

An appendix is simply evidence from your process journal that supports your claims within your report for each personal project criteria.

For your personal project report you are allowed a maximum of 10 pages containing carefully selected process journal extracts that provide evidence for each of the objectives/criteria.

A process journal extract may include:

- visual thinking diagrams
- bulleted lists
- charts
- short paragraphs
- notes
- timelines, action plans
- annotated illustrations
- annotated research
- artifacts from inspirational visits to museums, performances, galleries
- pictures, photographs, sketches
- up to 30 seconds of visual or audio material
- screenshots of a blog or website
- self- and peer-assessment feedback.

Your appendix could include the following possible process journal extracts to show evidence of all of the criteria.

Criterion A: Investigating	Creating a highly challenging goal. Subject-specific knowledge and prior learning reflection. Evaluation of sources. + more.
Criterion B: Planning	Specification, criteria for success. Gantt chart or other form of planning; reflection of how you have stuck to the planning time frame and goals. Process journal reflection on self-management skills, struggles, overcoming and so on. + more.
Criterion C: Taking action	Evidence of your product/outcome (photos, screenshots, extracts or 30 seconds of video of the product/outcome). Process journal reflections on thinking skills. Process journal reflections on communication and social skills. + more.
Criterion D: Reflecting	Evidence of your evaluation of the product/outcome against your criteria for success with justifications. Process journal reflections on extension of knowledge and understanding of topic and global contexts. Process journal reflections on your development as a learner.

CHAPTER SUMMARY KEY POINTS

- The process journal plays an important role in your personal project
- It should be uses for planning, recording information, exploring ideas, reflecting and evaluating your work
- Your process journal can be in any format – whatever you find most useful
- Take care selecting extracts for your final report. Remember you can use up to ten pages.

Investigating

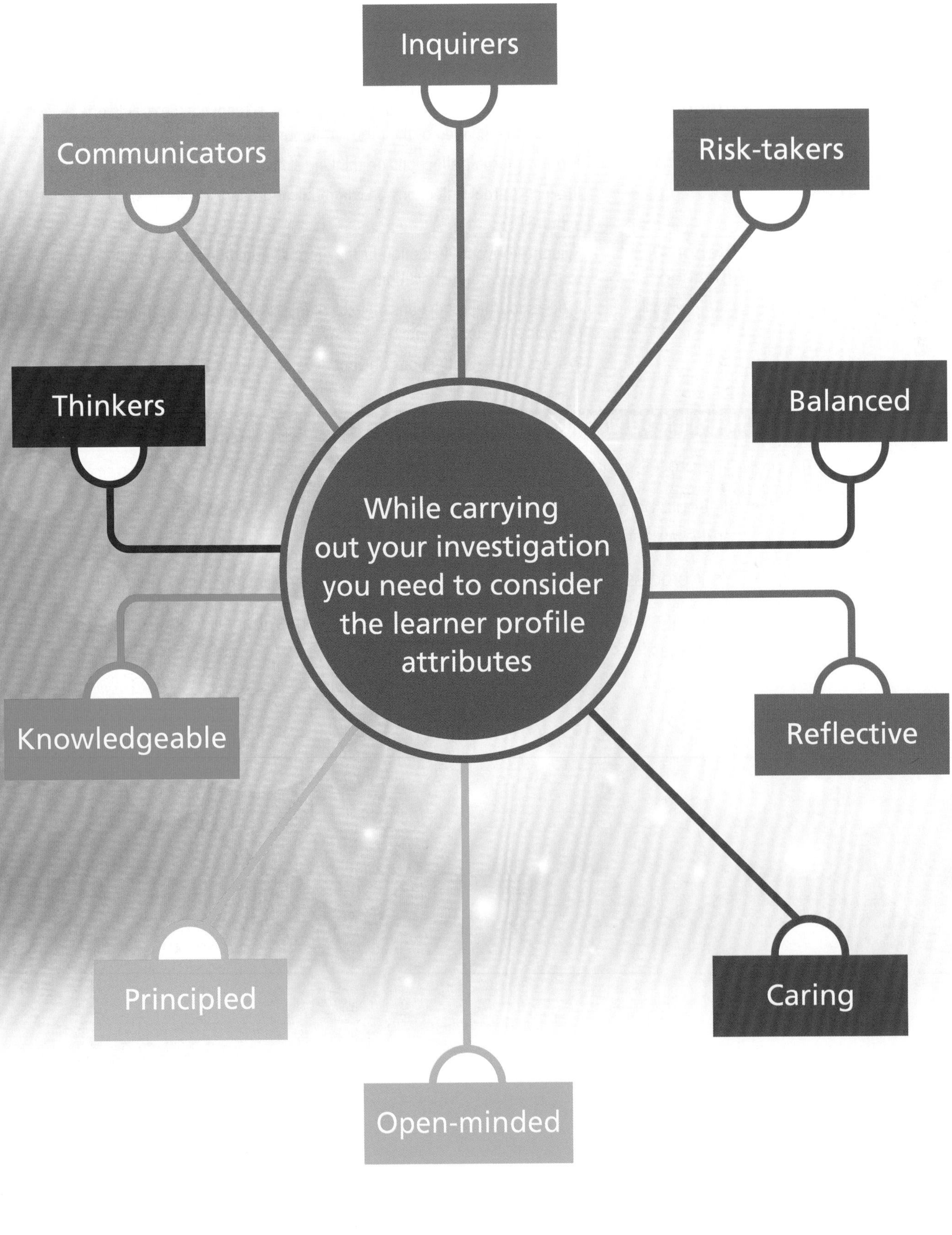

Inquirers
Communicators
Risk-takers
Thinkers
Balanced
While carrying out your investigation you need to consider the learner profile attributes
Knowledgeable
Reflective
Principled
Caring
Open-minded

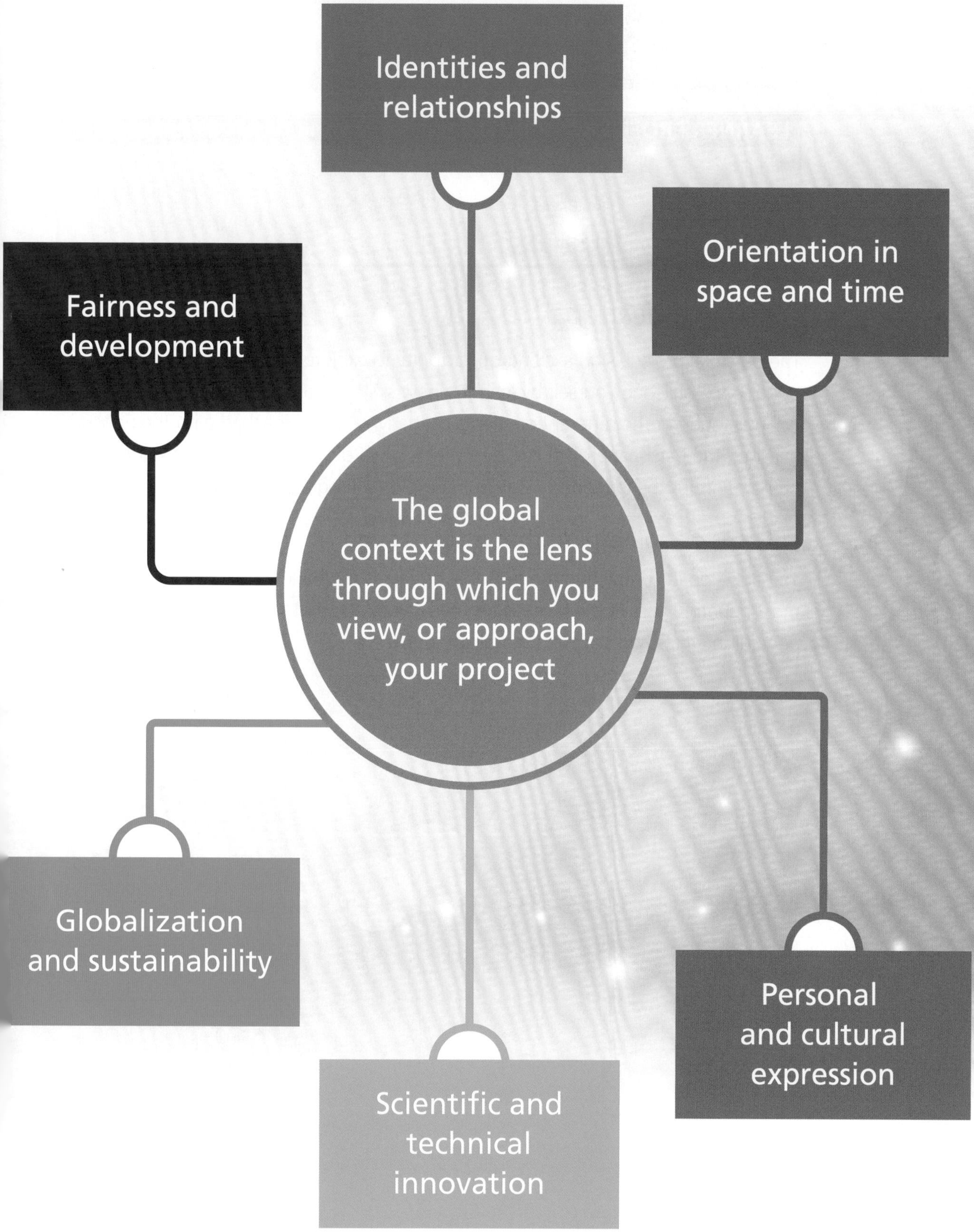

Identities and relationships
Orientation in space and time
Fairness and development
The global context is the lens through which you view, or approach, your project
Globalization and sustainability
Personal and cultural expression
Scientific and technical innovation

CHAPTER 3

Investigating

ATL skills

- Communication skills
- Organization skills
- Information literacy skills
- Media literacy skills
- Critical-thinking skills
- Creative-thinking skills
- Transfer skills

LEARNER PROFILE ATTRIBUTES

Inquirers	Communicators
Knowledgeable	Risk-takers
Thinkers	Reflective

Defining a clear goal

The personal project is an exciting opportunity to explore an area of personal interest but also to challenge yourself by learning new skills. In completing your project, you will pull together the different elements of the MYP. If approached with the right mindset, the personal project can be a highly rewarding experience – and good preparation for the Extended Essay in the Diploma Programme.

Focus on something that interests you

The first step in completing the personal project is to define a goal. This is often the most daunting part of the process for many students, so it might be helpful to reflect on your interests and skills, in the following activity.

ACTIVITY: WHAT INTERESTS ME?

Ask yourself the following questions to help you refine your ideas for your personal project.

What do I like doing in my spare time?

What are some of my hobbies or interests?

What are some of the things I do really well?

What would I like to do better?

What would I like to learn more about?

***Most importantly:* What can I see myself committing to for the next several months without losing interest?**

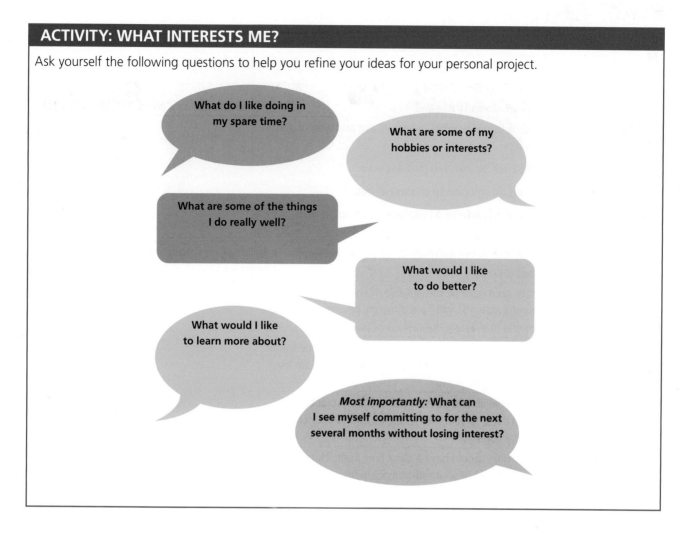

It is important to note that a topic is not the same thing as a goal. Your topic will be a broad theme, but your goal will be a specific action that you plan to undertake in relation to that theme. For example, your topic may be human cloning, but your goal could be to produce a journal article which considers the ethical implications of human cloning.

The end result of your goal must be a *product*. This could be a physical product such as a report, an original work of art, an invention, a science experiment or it could be a less tangible product like a performance, a presentation or an awareness campaign. Either way, you must provide *evidence* of your product within your process journal and report (for example, photographs, slides or video clips).

EXPERT TIP

If you choose to write a report as part of your product, you must still produce a separate report (whether in a written or oral format) in which you explicitly address the assessment criteria. If this is the case, it may be helpful to refer to the project report as the "reflective report" in order to avoid confusion and differentiate between the two project elements.

When choosing a goal, it is a good idea to ensure that it is a SMART goal. Copy and complete the following table:

S M A R T	**What does it mean?**	**Ideas for my own SMART goal(s)**
Specific	This is the who, what, when, where and why of your project. **Who** will be involved (besides you)? **What** do you plan to produce/achieve? **When** and **where** do you plan to complete your project? **Why** this particular goal? What is your personal motivation?	
Measurable	Your goal must be measurable. If your goal is not measurable, you will have difficulty developing relevant criteria to evaluate the success of your project.	
Achievable	Your goal should be achievable within the time frame you have, whilst still presenting the appropriate level of challenge.	
Relevant	Your goal should be relevant – to the project objectives, to your own interests and to your chosen global context.	
Timely	Your goal should have a clear time limit. This will help you in terms of your self-management.	

Demonstrating an appropriate level of challenge

When defining your goal, it is important to demonstrate an appropriate level of challenge. Ultimately, this can mean the difference between achieving the top levels of Criterion A, which specify that you must "define a **clear and highly challenging** goal and context for the project, based on personal interests". You will need to justify your goal as highly challenging in your report.

So while it may be tempting to play it safe and choose a project based on skills you already have, remember that as an IB learner you are encouraged to be a risk-taker!

Challenging goal	Highly challenging goal
A student documents his or her self-taught skills of photography.	A student documents his or her neighbourhood through a photography exhibition.
A student creates a durable bag using second-hand materials.	A student creates a range of bags using second-hand materials to exhibit at the local arts centre.
A student writes an article on a topic of interest for a journal (school/academic/ special interest) and submits it to an audience.	A student writes and publishes an original book-length feature on a topic of interest.

Why is this a highly challenging goal? Documenting a self-taught skill is certainly a challenging goal, but what makes the highly challenging goal is the way in which the product is presented. An exhibition allows you to demonstrate the ATL skill of communication; specifically, to communicate information and ideas effectively to audiences using a variety of media and formats.

Why is this a highly challenging goal? Again, the level of challenge here is best reflected in the way in which the product is presented.

Why is this a highly challenging goal? The highly challenging aspect of this goal is in the depth of research that would be required – not to mention the time commitment involved – to write a book-length feature. The student would also potentially have to communicate and collaborate with publishers and editors to be able to successfully achieve the second aspect of the goal, demonstrating further development of ATLs.

ACTIVITY: DEFINE YOUR GOAL

ATL skills

- Communication skills
  - Give and receive meaningful feedback
  - Negotiate ideas and knowledge with peers and teachers
- Organization skills
  - Set goals that are challenging and realistic

Now it's your turn. Define your goal for your personal project. Then in pairs, give your goal to your partner.

Read your partner's goal and question them about it in order to write a more challenging goal.

You could ask your partner some of the following questions:

- Is it specific enough?
- What is your criteria for evaluating the success of your project?
- What is your time frame? Is it achievable?
- Have you chosen the most appropriate and relevant global context?

You may wish to redefine your goal after answering some of these questions!

Identifying prior learning and subject-specific knowledge relevant to the project

If you have chosen a goal based on your personal interests, it is likely that you will bring a certain level of prior knowledge to the process. This could be knowledge you have gained through your MYP studies or through your personal hobbies and interests. It is important that you make explicit reference to this prior knowledge within your process journal and report, and that you explain clearly how this prior knowledge contributed to the creation of the product or achievement of the goal.

Reflecting on your prior learning and subject-specific knowledge demonstrates engagement with your topic and gives the assessor a context for your choice. You will not be able to demonstrate the highest levels of Criterion A without addressing this key element.

ACTIVITY: KNOW-WANT TO KNOW-LEARNT

ATL skills

- Transfer skills
  - Apply skills and knowledge in unfamiliar situations

Copy and complete the first two columns of the KWL chart opposite. You will revisit this activity in Chapter 6 when you reflect on what you have learnt throughout the process.

K: What do you already KNOW about your chosen topic?

W: What do you WANT to learn through your process of inquiry?

L: What have you LEARNT? What knowledge have you gained or skills have you developed?

K	W	L

Choosing a global context for the project

After deciding on a goal, the next most important step in the personal project process is to select a **global context**. The global context is the lens through which you view, or approach, your project, and often it will direct your line of inquiry.

It is important to note that more than one global context may be relevant to your chosen topic, but you should settle on the one which is most relevant to your project's goal and final outcome. Reflecting meaningfully on one global context is better than superficially addressing several global contexts.

Think–Pair–Share

Read the information provided in the table on page 31. In pairs, think of some examples of personal projects you might like to explore for each of the global contexts. You need to think about what the product and outcome might be too. What is the best outcome for the global context? Share your ideas with your partner. Can they suggest other global contexts you could use? What do they think of your product and outcome? Can they suggest any alternatives?

Global context	Examples of personal projects and their product/outcome
Identities and relationships  Explores: • identity • beliefs and values • personal, physical, mental, social and spiritual health • human relationships including families, friends, communities and cultures • what it means to be human	• Two sides of social networking → an awareness campaign about digital citizenship and cyber bullying. • How online identities impact offline relationships → a research essay. • Keeping culinary traditions → a video series following family recipes with historical relevance. • The effect of mass media on teenage identity → a short film.
Orientation in space and time  Explores: • personal histories • homes and journeys • turning points in humankind • discoveries • explorations and migrations of humankind • relationships between and the interconnectedness of individuals and civilizations from personal, local and global perspectives	• The Euclidean space perspective of the universe → a 3-D model. • Explorers in search of a new world → immigration over the ages through visual texts. • The *Mayflower* and the dream of religious freedom → a personal family history. • Charting a family history through archives → a representational statue.
Personal and cultural expression  Explores: • the ways in which we discover and express ideas, feelings, nature, culture, beliefs and values • the ways in which we reflect on, extend and enjoy our creativity • our appreciation of the aesthetic	• Video games as a form of cultural expression → a short film using five video games that shows how they are an expression of our culture. • The art of Manga in Japanese culture → a Japanese anime and a survey of the understanding of my peers. • Culture and self-expression through dance at the local community arts centre → a performance.
Scientific and technical innovation  Explores: • the natural world and its laws • interaction between people and the natural world • how humans use their understanding of scientific and technological advances on communities and environments • the impact of environments on human activity • how humans adapt environments to their needs	• Nanofibers build stronger bikes → a prototype bike with nanofibers. • What's the matter with the anti-matter? → an informational talk. • Why are genetics and genomics important to my health? → a media presentation. • Can stem cells replace organ transplants? → an investigative report.
Globalization and sustainability  Explores: • the interconnectedness of human-made systems and communities • the relationship between local and global processes • how local experiences mediate the global • the opportunities and tensions provided by world-interconnectedness • the impact of decision-making on humankind and the environment	• The struggle for water in developing countries → an awareness campaign. • The impact of the financial crises of Europe and the European Economic Community on the United States → a visual presentation. • Education as the tool to change the future of Peru → a workshop for adults. • The role of developing countries in protecting the tropical rainforest → a collection of slides.
Fairness and development  Explores: • rights and responsibilities • the relationship between communities • sharing finite resources with other people and with other living things • access to equal opportunities • peace and conflict resolution	• Supporting fair trade: cocoa trade in Ghana → an awareness campaign for our school restaurant/cafeteria to promote fair trade. • Open-market economies and their role in fair trade → a talk for students. • Exploring the intersections of race and inequality → a radio broadcast. • Asylum seekers and their right to live like us → a painting.

The global context should not be an add-on at the end but should form an integral part of your inquiry from the very early stages of the process.

An example of how your inquiry process may be affected by the global context you choose is shown here:

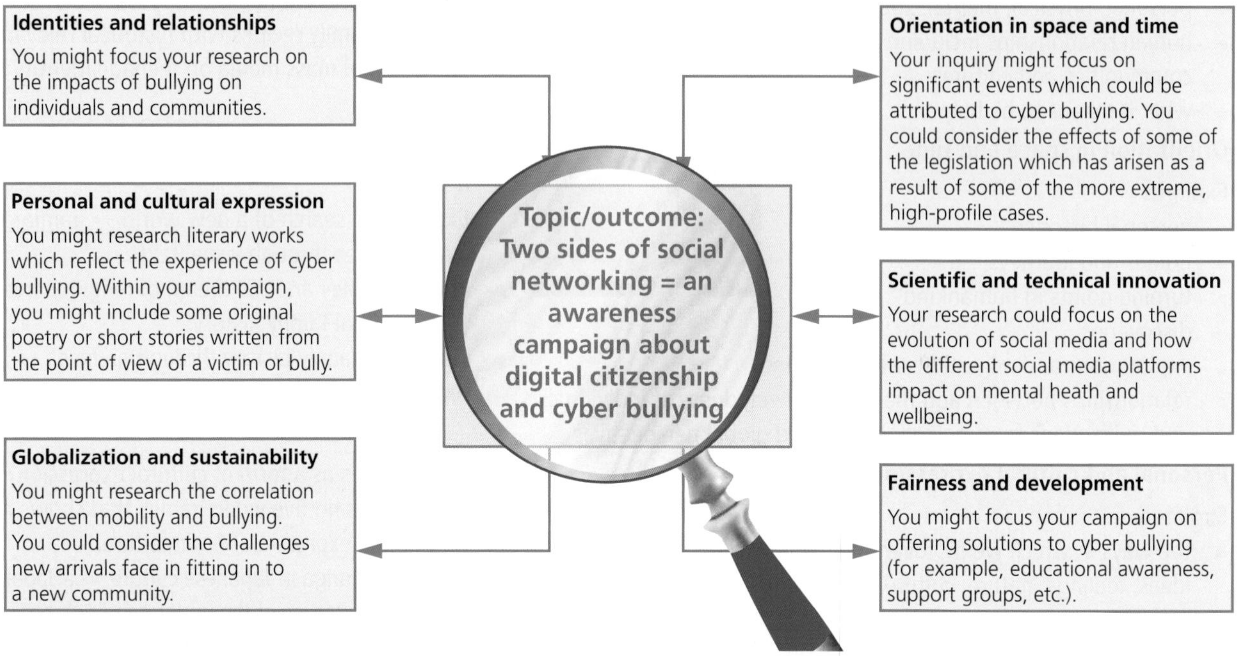
Identities and relationships
You might focus your research on the impacts of bullying on individuals and communities.
Personal and cultural expression
You might research literary works which reflect the experience of cyber bullying. Within your campaign, you might include some original poetry or short stories written from the point of view of a victim or bully.
Globalization and sustainability
You might research the correlation between mobility and bullying. You could consider the challenges new arrivals face in fitting in to a new community.
Topic/outcome: Two sides of social networking = an awareness campaign about digital citizenship and cyber bullying
Orientation in space and time
Your inquiry might focus on significant events which could be attributed to cyber bullying. You could consider the effects of some of the legislation which has arisen as a result of some of the more extreme, high-profile cases.
Scientific and technical innovation
Your research could focus on the evolution of social media and how the different social media platforms impact on mental heath and wellbeing.
Fairness and development
You might focus your campaign on offering solutions to cyber bullying (for example, educational awareness, support groups, etc.).

Defining a global context

ACTIVITY: GLOBAL CONTEXT

ATL skills

- Transfer skills
  - Change the context of an inquiry to gain different perspectives

In groups, place each of your personal project ideas in the centre, and think about how the global context changes your goal.

ATL skills

Throughout the completion of your personal project, you will be demonstrating a number of the Approaches to Learning skills. You must reflect explicitly and meaningfully on which skills you have demonstrated – and how – in your process journal and report.

The following table can help you visualize possible alignment of the ATL skill clusters with the objective strands. This is not the only way to align ATL skills with the objectives; there is flexibility regarding how and where you evidence the skills that you have demonstrated throughout the project, but you must make this explicit within your process journal and your report.

Objectives	**ATL skills clusters**	Affective skills: Mindfulness, perseverance, emotional management, self-motivation and resilience
Objective A: Investigating		
Define a clear goal and a global context for the project, based on personal interests	Collaboration Critical-thinking Creative-thinking	
Identify prior learning and subject-specific knowledge relevant to the project Demonstrate research skills	Information literacy Media literacy Transfer	
Objective B: Planning		
Develop criteria for the product/outcome	Collaboration Organization Critical-thinking Creative-thinking	
Plan and record the development process of the project Demonstrate self-management skills	Collaboration Organization Reflection	
Objective C: Taking action		
Create a product/outcome in response to the goal, context and criteria	Organization Critical-thinking Creative-thinking	
Demonstrate thinking skills Demonstrate communication and social skills	Communication Collaboration Critical-thinking Creative-thinking Transfer	
Objective D: Reflecting		
Evaluate the quality of the product/outcome against the criteria	Communication Reflection	
Reflect on how completing the project has extended their knowledge and understanding of the topic and the global context		
Reflect on their development as IB learners through the project		

EXPERT TIP

It is a good idea to label your process journal entries with the ATL skill or skills that are best demonstrated in each entry. This sign-posting can help the assessor, who will be looking for clear and explicit evidence of the ATL skills that you have developed throughout the project. Some of these skills can be reflected on in further detail in the report.

Learner profile attributes

Throughout your MYP studies you will have developed as an IB learner. Just as you will have reflected on which ATL skills you have developed throughout the project, you should also reflect on which of the learner profile attributes you have demonstrated, and *how*. For example, have you been a risk-taker? Has your topic required you to be open-minded? Have you become more reflective? Although you will address this most explicitly in relation to Criterion D, your development as an IB learner, which includes the learner profile traits and the approaches to learning (ATL) skills, is an element which lies at the heart of the project and should be considered and reflected on from the initial stages of the process.

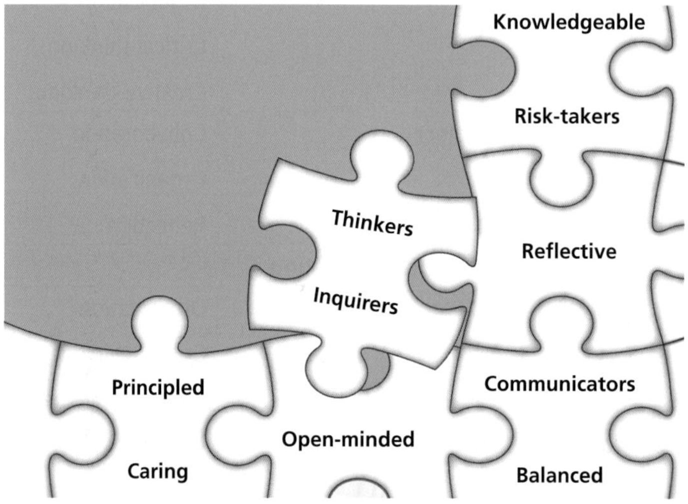
Knowledgeable
Risk-takers
Thinkers
Reflective
Inquirers
Principled
Communicators
Open-minded
Caring
Balanced

The IB learner profile

We will cover the learner profile attributes in more detail in Chapter 6, but it is important to start thinking about the learner profile attributes you demonstrate throughout your personal project.

Research skills

It is important to remember that the personal project is an inquiry-based project; therefore, your project must involve a certain level of research. Even creative projects should include some outside research. For example, if you are writing a collection of short stories based around a particular theme, you could research, among other things, notable authors who have written about similar themes, characteristics of the short story genre or the publishing process. However original the end product may be, you should demonstrate evidence of research and inquiry throughout the process, and this must be documented in your process journal and report.

Prior knowledge alone is not enough to demonstrate *breadth* of inquiry. Therefore, you will need to seek out other sources of information, including primary and secondary sources. Examples of primary sources might include, but are not limited to, images, interviews, survey data, results of experiments or field work. Secondary sources might include books, websites, journal articles or other published media. Depending on the type of project you undertake, you will likely use a combination of primary and secondary sources. There is no set number of sources which you must use as this will depend on the nature of the project itself.

Evidence of your research should be embedded throughout the project; a bibliography in and of itself is not sufficient enough to show *depth* of research. Within your process journal and your report, you should show evidence of your evaluation of sources. Using the OPVL (Origin, Purpose, Value and Limitation) method for evaluating sources, which you may be familiar with through your studies in Individuals and Societies, might be useful. Most importantly, you should reflect on how you have applied what you have learnt from your research to the product itself.

Origin	**Purpose**	**Value**	**Limitation**
Where does the source come from? When was the information published or posted? Who is the author, publisher, source, or sponsor? Are the author's credentials or organizational affiliations given? What are they?	What is the purpose of the source? What perspective is the author trying to convey? Is the purpose clear? Is the information fact, opinion or propaganda? Does the point of view appear objective or impartial?	How useful is the source? How can it be applied to my project? Has the information been reviewed or referred? Can you verify the information in another source?	How reliable is the source? Is it objective or subjective? Are there political, institutional, religious, cultural, ideological or personal biases?

ACTIVITY: HOW RELIABLE ARE YOUR SOURCES?

ATL skills

- Information literacy skills
  - Collect, record and verify data
  - Identify primary and secondary sources
- Media literacy skills
  - Locate, organize, analyse, evaluate, synthesize and ethically use information from a variety of sources and media (including digital source media and online networks)

Consider one of your sources through the OPVL lens. How reliable is that source? Will you still use that source in the same way now you have reflected on its reliability?

It is important to keep detailed notes and records in your process journal of the sources that you use throughout your project; it is worth referring to the section on academic honesty in Chapter 7. When assessing your project, assessors will be looking for clear evidence of research skills, which can include:

- creating research questions
- locating relevant, credible sources of information
- evaluating sources for reliability
- note-taking, summarizing or paraphrasing information
- acknowledging sources accurately
- creating (and including) a properly formatted bibliography.

Supervisor check-in

- Share your initial ideas with your supervisor. Your supervisor may be able to help you narrow your ideas down to a focused, specific goal.
- Discuss with your supervisor how you might focus your project through the different global context lenses. Which one seems most appropriate for your goal?
- Share your process journal with your supervisor. Your supervisor will need to see evidence of ongoing reflection, especially in relation to the ATLs.
- Share your research with your supervisor. If your supervisor is a subject expert, ask for their advice regarding further sources you might consult.

CHAPTER SUMMARY KEY POINTS

- The first objective of the personal project is Investigating.
- The first step in the investigation process is to choose a topic that interests you but also allows you to learn something new or develop a new skill.
- Once you have chosen a topic, you will need to define a clear and challenging goal.
- Goals should be SMART:
  - Specific
  - Measurable
  - Achievable
  - Relevant
  - Timely.
- You should identify any prior knowledge you bring with you to the project. This could include knowledge you have gained or skills you have developed through your MYP studies or outside of the classroom setting.
- You must choose a global context through which to focus your project. The global context should serve as a lens for your inquiry. The global contexts are:
  - Identities and relationships
  - Personal and cultural expression
  - Globalization and sustainability
  - Orientation in space and time
  - Scientific and technical innovation
  - Fairness and development

- Throughout the project, you will demonstrate several of the approaches to learning. You should reflect on these in your process journal and report.
- You will develop as an IB learner throughout the project. You should reflect on which of the learner profile traits the project allows you to demonstrate:
  - Inquirers
  - Knowledgeable
  - Thinkers
  - Communicators
  - Principled
  - Open-minded
  - Caring
  - Risk-takers
  - Balanced
  - Reflective
- The personal project provides you with an opportunity to develop and demonstrate research skills. Even creative projects should involve some level of research or inquiry.
- As part of the research process, you will need to show evidence of your evaluation of sources. A helpful tool is the OPVL method:
  - Origin
  - Purpose
  - Value
  - Limitation.

Planning

It is important to carefully plan each stage of your personal project. You will need to use **affective**, **cognitive** and **metacognitive** skills to do this.

AFFECTIVE SKILLS

Affective skills include your ability to manage your own time and be self-motivated, as well as being focused, resilient and persevering.

COGNITIVE SKILLS

Cognitive skills include your memory, problem-solving and attention skills.

METACOGNITIVE SKILLS

Metacognitive skills are essential for planning, as they include thinking about how to approach a task, strategies for problem solving and self-assessment.

CHAPTER 4

Planning

ATL skills

- Creative-thinking skills
- Organization skills
- Critical-thinking skills
- Reflection skills
- Collaboration skills

LEARNER PROFILE ATTRIBUTES

Thinkers	Balanced
Open-minded	Reflective
Caring	

EXPERT TIP

Think ahead to your Personal Project Exhibition. What do you want to show your audience? What sort of quality do you want to present at your Personal Project Exhibition? Use this mental image to guide how you create your specifications so you can visualize just what each specification will lead to.

Within this chapter you will come to understand just how important regular upkeep of your process journal is. Planning for your personal project is a continual process of strategically thinking ahead as well as reflecting on what you have achieved thus far in order to make informed decisions. A reminder: make sure in your process journal you make this continual process visible.

Developing criteria for the product/outcome

Now that you have set your goal, defined the global context for your project and engaged in extensive research, you need to transfer this into criteria for success for your product/outcome.

ACTIVITY: DEVELOPING YOUR PRODUCT/OUTCOME

ATL skills

- Creative-thinking skills
  - Consider multiple alternatives, including those that might be unlikely or impossible
- Organization skills
  - Plan short- and long-term assignments; meet deadlines

In order to develop criteria for your product/outcome, you firstly need to develop a set of specifications for your product/outcome.

When developing your specifications ask yourself the following questions:

- How will I know when I have achieved my goal?
- How can I judge the quality of my product/outcome?
- How will I know that I have effectively transferred my prior learning and subject-specific knowledge to the creation of my product/outcome?
- How will I know when I have successfully transferred the knowledge and skills I have acquired through research and collaboration to my product/outcome?
- How will I know that I have effectively represented the global context I have chosen through my product/outcome?

When developing your specifications you can consider the following options:

Message	Does your product/outcome need to convey a particular message? How will you know when you have effectively delivered this message? What impact do you want your product/outcome to have?		
Function	What must your product/outcome do? What is the purpose of your product/outcome?		
Target audience	Who is your product/outcome for? What is the target user's age, gender, socio-economic background?		
Language	What language needs do you need to consider when making your product/ outcome?		
Aesthetics	Consider: appearance size	 style colour shape/form	 texture pattern layout, and so on.
Environmental considerations	Where will your product/outcome be used? How will the design directly or indirectly impact the environment?		
Cost	Is there a maximum cost? Do you need to keep this within a budget?		
Cultural considerations	What cultural considerations do you need to consider in order to be respectful of cultural differences?		
Materials	What materials are available? What properties will the materials have?		
Resources	What resources are available? Are there limitations as to how this can be created?		
Practicalities	Are there any specific size requirements or restrictions that need to be considered? What spatial factors need to be considered?		

This is just an idea of some of the types of considerations you can make for your product/outcome. By all means think bigger and beyond these to the unique qualities of your project.

Qualitative and quantifiable

When developing criteria for success, it is important to consider the distinction between "qualitative" and "quantifiable" evaluation methods. When you have put your goal into action and created your product/outcome, you will be given the opportunity through reflection to evaluate the quality of your product/outcome by measuring the success of your project. Thinking in terms of qualitative methods of evaluation and quantifiable methods of evaluation you will be assured that you are thoroughly considering the multiple possibilities of just what a successful product/outcome is.

Quantifiable evaluation methods focus on what can be measured through the use of facts, raw data and what is tangibly obvious in your product/outcome. Some examples of quantifiable data evaluation methods embedded within your product/outcome could be the size, length, width and depth, types of resources used and the quantity of your product/outcome.

Qualitative evaluation methods focus on what is not easily measured by reducing to numbers. Qualitative evaluation methods are what is not necessarily tangibly obvious in your product/outcome. Some examples of qualitative evaluation methods embedded within your product/outcome could be the message, how it is designed specifically for a target audience or context, and how the product/outcome is designed to make others feel.

Developing criteria for success

It is important to develop thorough and well-considered criteria for your product/outcome. This criteria for success will provide a benchmark to ensure your product/outcome is an excellent response to your goal and global context. Your criteria for success will also provide a tool for constant self-assessment and evaluation of the quality of your product/outcome. There are many options for developing criteria for success. Choose from the following activities or create one that suits you and your project best.

Rubric

When you have your list of specifications outlined in your personal project process journal, you need to transfer each specification into a criteria for success. You will need to think deeply about what each specification will look like at the varying degrees of success.

ACTIVITY: RUBRIC

ATL skills

- Organization skills
  - Plan short- and long-term assignments; meet deadlines
  - Set goals that are challenging and realistic
  - Plan strategies and take action to achieve personal and academic goals
- Creative-thinking skills
  - Consider multiple alternatives, including those that might be unlikely or impossible

In your process journal, copy and complete the following criteria for success layout. The amount of specifications and descriptor levels is up to you. Keep in mind that you want your criteria to be rigorous. Make sure you describe just how the criteria for your product/outcome will be rigorous. Rigorous means well considered and thoroughly thought through.

	Specification 1	Specification 2	Specification 3	Specification 4
Excellent				
Substantial				
Adequate				
Limited				

Thinking deeply about the quality of your product/outcome at an excellent level, a substantial level, an adequate level and a limited level, ask yourself the following questions:

Excellent	If my product/outcome is excellent in quality, what exactly will I have achieved? What will the excellent qualities of my product/outcome be as described in my specifications? How will I have possibly exceeded my own expectations?
Substantial	If my product/outcome is substantial in quality, what exactly will I have achieved? What will the substantial qualities of my product/outcome be as described in my specifications? What is lacking from my product/outcome that makes it substantial, rather than excellent?
Adequate	If my product/outcome is adequate in quality, what exactly will I have achieved? What will the adequate qualities of my product/outcome be as described in my specifications? What is lacking from my product/outcome that makes it adequate, rather than substantial?
Limited	If my product/outcome is limited in quality, what exactly will I have achieved? What could go wrong that would cause my product/outcome to only achieve at a limited standard? What is lacking from my product/outcome that makes it limited, rather than adequate?

Explain clearly just what you will be looking for in each of these bands, because when you reach the reflecting criteria of the personal project journey you will need to measure the success of your project by self-assessing your product/outcome against the criteria for success that you have created, and you will need to justify each decision.

■ Example of criteria for success

For example, if you are creating a comic book within the global context of identities and relationships that reveals to your audience that ordinary people can demonstrate superhero qualities through selfless acts of service to others, two of your specifications and criteria might read:

Specification 1 (Quantifiable): The main character, Leonard the Parking Inspector, shows the audience that ordinary people, through heroic actions of selfless service to others, can demonstrate the qualities of a superhero using simply what they have available. In Leonard's case, a meter reader, clipboard, pencil and a piece of chalk.

Specification 2 (Qualitative): Readers are inspired to think of how they can demonstrate the qualities of a superhero using readily available, ordinary resources in their everyday lives.

These specifications can then be transferred to criteria for success at varying levels of success, clearly explaining what the quality of your product/outcome will be at each level of success.

	Specification 1: The main character, Leonard the Parking Inspector, shows the audience that ordinary people, through heroic actions of selfless service to others, can demonstrate the qualities of a superhero using simply what they have available. In Leonard's case, a meter reader, clipboard, pencil and a piece of chalk.	**Specification 2:** Readers are inspired to think of how they can demonstrate the qualities of a superhero using readily available, ordinary resources in their everyday lives.
7–8 Excellent	When surveyed, readers agreed that the plot twist at the end of the comic showed them as readers that if ordinary individuals use what is available to them in a selfless act of service, they can demonstrate the qualities of a superhero.	Readers were inspired to think of how their everyday lives and resources can be used to demonstrate the qualities of a superhero, and were able to explain how they might do this in a real-life and hypothetical situation.

5–6 Substantial	When surveyed, readers mostly agreed that the plot twist at the end of the comic showed them as readers that if ordinary individuals use what is available to them in a selfless act of service, they can demonstrate the qualities of a superhero. What was lacking was a realistic setting and realistic dialogue that the audience could relate to.	Readers were mostly inspired to think of how their everyday lives and resources can be used to demonstrate the qualities of a superhero and were able to explain how they might do this in a real-life and hypothetical situation. However, the qualities given the everyday resources used in the comic were unrealistic, thus limiting their inspiration.
3–4 Adequate	When surveyed, readers thought that the plot twist at the end of the comic showed them as readers that given the right setting and circumstances, if ordinary individuals use what is available to them in a selfless act of service, they can demonstrate the qualities of a superhero. To make this realistic, what was lacking was a realistic setting and realistic dialogue that the audience could relate to within a familiar context.	Readers were somewhat inspired to think of how their everyday lives and resources can be used to demonstrate the qualities of a superhero, although they struggled to explain how they might do this in a hypothetical situation, let alone a real-life situation. The qualities given the everyday resources used in the comic were unrealistic, thus limiting their inspiration.
1–2 Limited	When surveyed, readers thought that the plot twist at the end of the comic did not demonstrate that they as readers and ordinary individuals can use what is available to them in a selfless act of service and demonstrate the qualities of a superhero. The readers believed the setting and dialogue was out of touch from the audience and they could not relate to this, even within a familiar context.	Readers were unfortunately not inspired to think of how their everyday lives and resources can be used to demonstrate the qualities of a superhero, as they struggled to explain how they might do this in a hypothetical situation, let alone a real-life situation. The qualities given the everyday resources used in the comic were unrealistic, thus limiting their inspiration and ability to be inspired within a real-life scenario.

These specifications have focused on the **message** of the comic book; there will need to be specifications that address the aesthetics, resources, language and so on. As you can see, this approach to developing criteria not only plans for product/outcome success, but also plans for collaboration and social skills through the use of a survey in order to gather meaningful feedback. Each project is unique, so develop criteria that is unique to your goal and criteria that fits the purpose and intent of your goal.

Think–Pair–Share

Are the two example specifications provided here examples of quantifiable or qualitative methods of evaluation?

Remember, this is just an example of possibilities, your own specifications and criteria for success should be project specific and incorporate both qualitative and quantifiable methods of evaluation.

You can also make the criteria levels unique to your product/outcome for greater personalization. For example, if you are creating a comic book your levels could be labelled:

Excellent project

KAPOW!

The comic book has addressed all your criteria and had just the impact you wished it would – Kapow! – totally awesome outcome.

Substantial project

Hurrah!

The comic book has addressed most of your criteria – Hurrah! – however, it hasn't quite received the impact you hoped for.

Adequate project

Meh!

The comic book has addressed some of your criteria, but none of the impact you hoped for, it's just Meh!

Limited project

epic fail

The comic book has barely addressed your criteria and has made zero impact – it's an epic fail.

> **EXPERT TIP**
>
> When you begin to take action and create your product/outcome, consistently refer to your criteria for success – this is how you will create the best possible product/outcome. Take time to think about the qualities and characteristics of your product/outcome and how you can describe these in project unique language. Have fun, take your time playing with project-specific language!

A reminder, the process of learning is filled with failure. This is not a negative, but rather, a positive. If we reflect on the what, how and why of failure we can turn this into a powerful and often unforgettable learning experience. The focus of the personal project is on the process – if things do go awry and you experience an "epic fail", choose to reflect on this and look for ways that you can learn from this experience and grow as a resilient and knowledgeable learner.

Checklist

Another option for developing success criteria for your product/outcome could be in the form of checklists that you can logically structure in order for your project to be successful. Something to continuously consider, the criteria for project success needs to be rigorous, that is, well considered and thoroughly thought through.

ACTIVITY: CHECKLIST

ATL skills

- Critical-thinking skills
  - Analyse complex concepts and projects into their constituent parts and synthesize them to create new understanding
  - Identify obstacles and challenges; identify trends and forecast possibilities
- Reflection skills
  - Consider personal learning strategies – what can I do to become a more efficient and effective learner?
  - Demonstrate flexibility in the selection and use of learning strategies

To create a checklist you will need to apply your logical thinking skills and map each part carefully in order to plan for project success. Begin with a mind map to help organize your thinking process. Use this as a tool to begin to think about the qualities and requirements of your product/outcome.

■ Example of a mind map

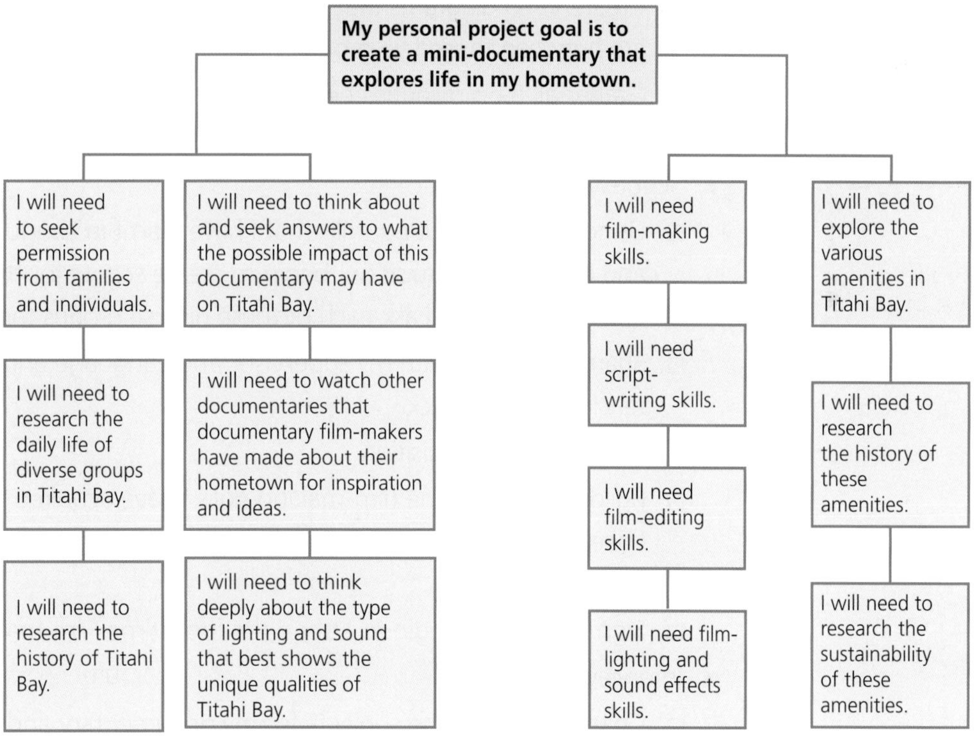
My personal project goal is to create a mini-documentary that explores life in my hometown.
I will need to seek permission from families and individuals.
I will need to research the daily life of diverse groups in Titahi Bay.
I will need to research the history of Titahi Bay.
I will need to think about and seek answers to what the possible impact of this documentary may have on Titahi Bay.
I will need to watch other documentaries that documentary film-makers have made about their hometown for inspiration and ideas.
I will need to think deeply about the type of lighting and sound that best shows the unique qualities of Titahi Bay.
I will need film-making skills.
I will need script-writing skills.
I will need film-editing skills.
I will need film-lighting and sound effects skills.
I will need to explore the various amenities in Titahi Bay.
I will need to research the history of these amenities.
I will need to research the sustainability of these amenities.

From this point of mind-mapping your ideas, you can logically structure these into the must haves for your product/outcome to be successful.

- Impact brainstorm
- Research
- Script-writing
- Film-making skill acquisition
- Interviews
- Post-production skill acquisition

Then to ensure that your checklist demonstrates rigour – well considered and thoroughly thought through – you can add descriptions to your checklist.

- Impact brainstorm
  - ☐ Brainstorm types of lighting and sound unique to my hometown by spending time at Titahi Bay just listening and recording the sounds at various times of the day. ☐
  - ☐ Watch other documentaries that film-makers have made about their town and take notes on my observation of the lighting and sound they have used to best reflect daily life in their hometown. ☐
  - ☐ Create a SOAR chart that unpacks the impact I want my documentary to have. ☐
- Research
  - ☐ Create a questionnaire that I can deliver to my neighbours and members of the Titahi Bay community to gather ideas of the type of impact they want my documentary to have. ☐
  - ☐ Find five diverse groups that live in Titahi Bay and brainstorm the qualities and characteristics of these diverse groups. ☐
  - ☐ Create Venn diagrams that show the differences and similarities that are between these five groups. ☐
  - ☐ Gather all the similarities between these diverse groups and use these as the main theme that runs through my documentary. ☐
- Script-writing
  - ☐ Using my script-writing skills that I have learnt in Language and Literature and Language Acquisition, begin to create scripts for the types of questions that I will ask each of these diverse groups for my documentary. ☐
  - ☐ Share my scripts with my supervisor and Language and Literature teacher for feedback. ☐
- Film-making skill acquisition
  - ☐ Building on from the film-making skills I have acquired in Arts – Media, I need to work through Stages 3–5 of the online tutorials for Abode Premiere. ☐
  - ☐ Sign up for and begin to attend the lunchtime Film-making Club. ☐
- Interviews
  - ☐ Collaborate with the subjects for my documentary and book/schedule appropriate times to meet with them. ☐
  - ☐ Conduct the interviews and film each of these for my documentary using the camera angles and film techniques I have learnt in the Abode Premiere online tutorials and the lunchtime Film-making Club. ☐
- Post production skill acquisition
  - ☐ Edit the footage I have gathered. ☐
  - ☐ Layer the music and sound effects that I have chosen at the beginning of my documentary film-making journey. ☐
  - ☐ Create cover art and upload to Vimeo. ☐

As you progress in taking action and creating your product/outcome, tick off the items as you fulfill them. As obstacles arise and you may need to re-adjust your checklist, document this in your process journal and explain how you have solved problems and overcome obstacles.

Single-point rubric

If you are a learner who likes to collaborate with others and receive continual feedback, perhaps from a family member, friend, mentor or a member of the client/target audience of your project, you can create success criteria in the form of a single-point rubric.

ACTIVITY: SINGLE-POINT RUBRIC

ATL skills

- Critical-thinking skills
  - Analyse complex concepts and projects into their constituent parts and synthesize them to create new understanding
  - Identify obstacles and challenges; identify trends and forecast possibilities
- Collaboration skills
  - Take responsibility for one's own actions
  - Give and receive meaningful feedback

A single-point rubric only includes criteria for success at the highest level. The goal of the single-point rubric is to provide a structure for self-assessment, peer-assessment, mentor-assessment or supervisor-assessment to give targeted feedback on areas that need working on and also ways that you have exceeded your own criteria. Create a table similar to the example below.

Example of single-point rubric

For example, if you are writing a short story that highlights the impact of bullying via social media, your single-point rubric could look like this:

Needs improvement	Success criteria	Above and beyond
	Structure The opening paragraph of my short story grabs the reader's attention and establishes the context of the story. The story follows a logical plot sequence that includes some kind of rising action, climax, falling action, and resolution. The closing paragraph links back to the opening and uses the unresolved style, leaving my readers to think about impact of bullying via social media.	
	Ideation The story contains enough exposition about the characters, setting and context so that no important questions are left unanswered. The story clearly explains the significantly negative issue of bullying via social media so that the reader fully understands that for a person to have a healthy sense of self (my global context is identities and relationships) they need to know they can rise above bullying and, regardless of what has been said, they can hold their head up high.	

As you take action and create your product/outcome, choose strategic points throughout the creating process to seek feedback from family, friends, mentors, your supervisor or any other person or group of people who can offer you accurate and targeted feedback. Giving and receiving meaningful feedback is an important part of successfully engaging in the personal project.

The benefit of the single-point rubric for your planning is that you are not only planning for product/outcome success, but also strategically planning for collaboration with others in order to receive meaningful feedback.

EXPERT TIP

As you can see, there are several ways that you can develop success criteria in a rigorous and meaningful way. The key is to select, or create, the one that best suits your way of organizing and planning and the approach that best suits your product/outcome.

And remember, when you begin to take action and create your product/outcome, consistently refer to your criteria for success – this is how you will create the best possible product/outcome. Continual reflection and self-assessment is one of the many keys to personal project success.

Plan and record the development process

Drawing together your investigating and your criteria for success, you now need to create a detailed and accurate plan for the creation of your product/outcome **and for the completion of your personal project.**

What you create in this section of your personal project journey will need to be continually reflected on and most likely adjusted in response to the creation of your product/outcome as you take action.

It is essential that you create an achievable plan for your personal project. This requires you to forward plan and take into account the time frame, resources and materials that you need in order to create the product/outcome.

There are several ways you can create and present a detailed and accurate plan and record of the development process of the project. When choosing one or several methods for planning and recording the development process of your personal project, choose the method that suits you best.

Gantt chart

ACTIVITY: GANTT CHART

ATL skills

- Organization skills
  - Plan short- and long-term assignments; meet deadlines
  - Set goals that are challenging and realistic
- Collaboration skills
  - Take responsibility for one's own actions

One of the ways that you can plan and record the development process of your personal project is by creating a Gantt chart. Put simply, a Gantt chart is a useful way to plan for a large project. Create a table similar to the example below.

Simply place in the left-hand column all the steps, in logical and time-bound order, that need to be completed in order to create your product/outcome and complete your personal project. Then along the top, place your time frame. You can use school weeks or specific dates – the choice is up to you.

Colour in the correct spaces for the time frame in which you wish to achieve this goal. You can change the colour once you have completed this step, or make notations if you are unable to keep to the time frame and explain the reasons why.

Your Gantt chart is a way that you can forward plan, a way to gather a big picture of what needs to be achieved within the allocated time frame as outlined in your SMART goal, and it is also flexible to help you adjust your planning based on possible interruptions and setbacks.

Objective	Resources	Week 10	Week 1	Week 2	Week 3	Week 1	Week 2	Week 3	Week 4	Week 5	Week 6	Week 7	Week 8	Week 9	Week 10
Investigation:															
Define Community Project goal	Seqta – Learn and individual devices														
Define research															
Research process	Primary and secondary sources														
Evaluation of sources															
Planning:															
Assign roles for completion															
Create rubric for success															
Refine Gantt chart															
Taking Action:															
Capture photographs	iPhones, individual devices, transport, internet connection, Instagram Text-Write and Tumblr apps.														
Create quotes and hashtags															
Record progress in Process Journal															
Edit images and synthesize															
Double-check and get group feedback															
Publish on Tumblr															
Reflecting:															
Evaluate against rubric for success	Seqta – Learn and individual devices														
Write TEDx-style talk script															
Create Appendix and Bibliography															
Double-check, edit and refine															
Presenting:															
Deliver TEDx-style talk for report	Projector, individual devices, recording device														

Kanban board

Another way of planning and recording the development process of your personal project is by creating a Kanban board. Like the Gantt chart, this is a useful way to plan for a large project.

ACTIVITY: KANBAN BOARD

ATL skills

- Organization skills
  - Plan short- and long-term assignments; meet deadlines
  - Set goals that are challenging and realistic
- Collaboration skills
  - Take responsibility for one's own actions

A Kanban board helps you plan for and organize progress by simply visualizing what needs to be done; it shows what is "in progress" and what "has been accomplished". Use sticky notes on paper, a whiteboard or utilize one of the many digital software packages available to create a Kanban board.

To do	Doing	Done

You will find that as more and more of your tasks are met you can visualize the "done" column of your Kanban board growing. So when the going gets a bit tough and perhaps motivation and time-management are becoming a bit tricky, this will give you the incentive to keep going and keep creating.

Make the most of a blend of analogue and digital. You may choose to allocate a section of a wall at home to a large scale Kanban board where you can track your progress. This is also a means of including your family and friends in the personal project process as they can celebrate your achievements and progress with you.

Scrum board

Another means of planning for the record and development of your process is through a Scrum board.

ACTIVITY: SCRUM BOARD

ATL skills

- Organization skills
  - Plan short- and long-term assignments; meet deadlines
  - Set goals that are challenging and realistic
- Collaboration skills
  - Take responsibility for one's own actions
  - Give and receive meaningful feedback
- Reflection skills
  - Consider personal learning strategies – what can I do to become a more efficient and effective learner?
  - Demonstrate flexibility in the selection and use of learning strategies

The Scrum board is similar to the Kanban board, but is more descriptive and broken down into smaller chunks. Study the explanation below and then create your own Scrum board.

User story

The first column begins with what is called the "User story". This is simply a statement explaining the "what" and "why" of each of the steps of your personal project.

Each User story can be created using the following sentence prompts:

I want to … so that I can …

For example: *I want to prepare my canvases, so that I can begin the pencil outlines of the foreground images of my painting.*

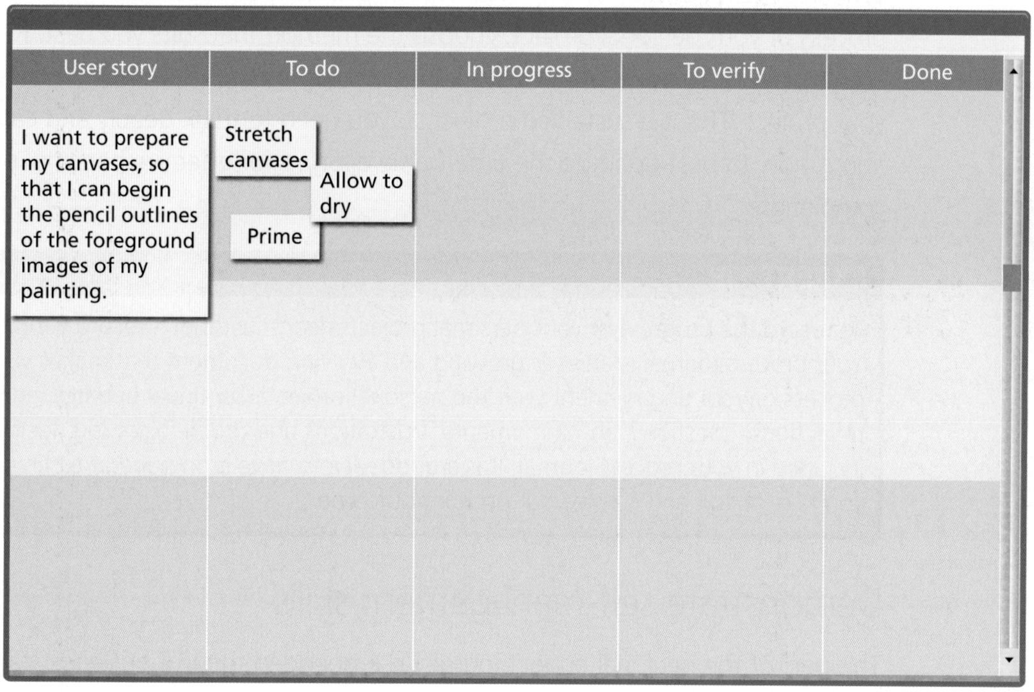
User story
To do
In progress
To verify
Done
I want to prepare my canvases, so that I can begin the pencil outlines of the foreground images of my painting.
Stretch canvases
Allow to dry
Prime

To do

The second column is where you simply bullet point what needs to be done in order to achieve the goal of your User story.

For example:

- stretch canvases
- prime
- allow to dry

In progress

The third column is where you shift your To do sticky note or text box to the "In progress" column. If you have come across challenges, jot these down, and going back to your To do list, add what you need to do in order to overcome these challenges. This is a fluid board that visualizes your process based on both your setbacks and your progress.

To verify

The fourth column is where you verify your progress. This is a strategic and intentional point to self-assess your progress against your success criteria. Using your rigorous criteria for success (that should be continuously referred to throughout the process) self-assess what you have achieved thus far to ensure that you are aiming for the best possible outcome of your product/outcome. Seek feedback from your supervisor, peers, mentor, family and friends.

If you are not happy with your self-assessment, head back to your User story or To do list and think about what needs to be adjusted in order for you to improve. Repeat as necessary.

Done

Finally, the fifth and last column is where you move your To do sticky note or text box to visualize process success. Give yourself a pat on the back, high-five those closest by or post via social media the successful completion of one of your User stories!

Diary and calendar

Using your diary and calendar is another option for planning and recording the development process of your personal project. No doubt as MYP students you already do this as part of your regular life as a student and a self-managed learner. Building self-determined deadlines into your school or personal diary is another way in which you can plan and record the development process of your personal project. Remember, planning the development of your personal project is about forward thinking, planning and reflecting in order to make informed decisions.

When choosing one or several methods for planning and recording the development process of your personal project, choose the method that suits you best. Research and explore other ways of planning and recording the development process of your project. This is a sustained project so you need to think deeply and carefully about how to best optimize the time frame allotted for effective personal project completion.

EXPERT TIP

To record the progress of your personal project means just that – record your progress. Your process journal is an ever-growing and evolving document that makes visible the process of your engagement with the personal project. Continual updates, annotations, reflections, questions, ah-ha moments, frustrations and problem solving need to be included in your process journal. It is a good idea to have it on hand at all times while you take action and create your product/outcome.

Demonstrate self-management skills

This part of the personal project journey is embedded throughout each stage of the project.

Self-management skills are ways of organizing the actual project as well as organizing your state of mind.

In your process journal, ensure you document and make very visible the ways in which you have organized the personal project as well as organized your state of mind. Remember to include examples and scenarios in order to make sure your thinking is visible.

Organization skills include:

- meeting deadlines
- sticking to your goals
- making plans that are logically and sequentially efficient
- maintaining your process journal with regular updates
- selecting and using technology effectively and productively.

Through developing rigorous criteria for your product/outcome and planning and recording the process of your personal project, you will have the support mechanisms in place to meet deadlines that are logically and sequentially organized for optimal efficiency and to help you stick to your goals, all the while maintaining your process journal with regular updates. Remember to take risks and be open-minded to the variety of technology within your reach. Select and use technology in an effective and productive manner that is best suited to the needs of your project.

Affective skills include:

- Mindfulness – practise strategies to overcome distractions and maintain mental focus.

Mindfulness strategies empower you to focus your mental and physical energy onto a certain aspect of your personal project in such a way that you are not easily distracted by external distractors and can maintain mental focus.

As MYP students you have busy academic schedules. Along with this you most likely also have active social lives, both online and offline. When practising mindfulness strategies to overcome distractions and maintain mental focus, it is good to consider how you orientate yourself in both place and time.

ACTIVITY: MAINTAINING MENTAL FOCUS

ATL skills

- Organization skills
  - Plan short- and long-term assignments; meet deadlines
- Affective skills
  - Perseverance
  - Self-motivation
  - Resilience

Place: Set aside a location that has minimal distractions in order for you to intentionally position yourself in a location that supports you maintaining mental focus. Turn off your notifications. Unplug from social media. Actively organize yourself and your personal project resources in such a way that you can maintain mental focus.

Time: Refer consistently to your planning chart, be conscious of creating the time for a balanced approach to effective personal project completion. The entirety of the personal project should take around 25 hours to complete, make the most of each minute of these hours. Choose your best time of the day for optimal concentration and mental focus.

Perseverance: Demonstrate persistence and perseverance and help others demonstrate persistence and perseverance. This begins with a growth mindset. A growth mindset requires that we are optimistic and we have the tools to challenge faulty thinking when the project becomes challenging.

EXPERT TIP

Throughout the duration of your project you will undoubtedly come across points where you will need to persist and persevere. A learner with a growth mindset does not give up at this point; they simply stop, pause and reflect in order to reassess how to move forwards from there.

ACTIVITY: THE MoSCoW METHOD

ATL skills

- Collaboration skills
  - Take responsibility for one's own actions
- Reflection skills
  - Consider personal learning strategies
  - Demonstrate flexibility in the selection and use of learning strategies

An effective way of reassessing your progress and making decisive steps forward is to employ the MoSCoW method. Break down what you need to achieve into smaller chunks and break this down into what you "must do" and "should do" to achieve this goal, "could do" to go over and above and "won't do" to ensure optimal persistence and perseverance.

Must do	Should do	Could do	Won't do

Must do: Jot down what is absolutely essential for you to persevere and persist to achieve this goal.

Should do: Jot down what you should do to persevere and persist to achieve this goal.

Could do: Jot down what you could do to ensure you are working towards self-assessing your product/ outcome at an excellent level, even though you may be struggling to persist and persevere.

Won't do: Intentionally plan for blocking out distractions and hindrances to your persevering and persisting to complete this goal.

Seeing these small successes will help you to persist and persevere. Remember, personal project success is made up of multiple small successes that culminate into significant project success.

Self-motivation: Practise analysing and attributing causes for failure, and practise positive thinking.

Self-motivation requires habits of mind that focus on thinking about the big picture. At the beginning of your personal project you will have established your goal explaining why this project is important to you. When problems occur and you experience failure, it is a good idea to reflect back on why your project is important to you.

When attributing causes for failure, it is important to keep the positives in mind. It is a good idea to begin with listing what has gone well so far and then exploring from there the causes for failure. Once you have analysed and attributed the causes for failure, ensure you then refocus on the bigger picture of why persevering and persisting in this project is important to you.

When we experience failure in a large project it can be easy to go down a negative spiral of doubt, practising positive thinking can help build the growth mindset required for personal project success.

Reflection skills include:

- being **open-minded**, developing new skills, techniques and strategies for effective learning
- being **reflective** by keeping a journal to record reflections
- taking note of how your thinking is changing by using the "I used to think …" "Now I think …" sentence prompts
- being **principled** by identifying strengths and weaknesses of personal learning strategies (self-assessment).
- **taking risks** by trying new learning strategies and reflecting on the effectiveness of this new learning strategy.

Due to the sustained inquiry nature of the personal project it is beneficial to stop and pause at points along the way and reassess your progress, celebrate what you have achieved thus far and clarify the steps forward that you will take.

ACTIVITY: COMPASS POINTS VISIBLE THINKING ROUTINE

ATL skills

- Collaboration skills
  - Take responsibility for one's own actions
  - Give and receive meaningful feedback
- Reflection skills
  - Consider personal learning strategies
  - Demonstrate flexibility in the selection and use of learning strategies

The Compass Points visible thinking routine is an effective tool to calibrate your personal project situation and assess "where to go from here".

E = Excitements: What excites you about what you have achieved so far?

W = Worries: What have you found worrisome about your project progress so far?

N = Needs: What else do you need to find out, or skills do you need to acquire, to move forward?

S = Steps or Suggestions: What should your next step be? Show your peers, family or supervisor your Excitements, Worries and Needs – what suggestions do they have for you?

Information gathered from this reflection may mean you need to adjust your planning tools and criteria; this is fine, remember the personal project is a journey of continual reflection. In your process journal, make sure you document your reflection of your organization and self-management skills.

EXPERT TIP

Be honest – managing our state of mind is often one of the trickiest things to do. The more we reflect on our ability to organize ourselves and work on the best ways to manage our state of mind, the more we help ourselves and others.

Supervisor check-in

- Share your criteria for success with your supervisor and clarify the following with them in order to receive feedback. You can ask the question, "Does the criteria for success that I have created truly qualify as well considered and appropriately thought through criteria?"
- Share your approach to planning and recording the development of your personal project. Discuss with your supervisor how you can include them in your development process and how they can support you in keeping to the time frames that you have set.
- Share with your supervisor how you are demonstrating self-management skills by managing both your project and your state of mind. Your supervisor will no doubt have approaches to self-management that they can share with you.

CHAPTER SUMMARY KEY POINTS

- Develop a set of specifications for your product/outcome that can be transferred to criteria for success as a means of continual self-assessment and evaluation of your final product/outcome.
- Transfer your specifications to criteria for success. Possible approaches to developing criteria for success include:
  - rubric
  - checklist
  - single-point rubric.
- Develop approaches to planning and recording the development process of your personal project, ensuring that this is documented in your process journal. Possible approaches include:
  - Gantt chart
  - Kanban board
  - Scrum board
  - Diary/calendar.
- Continuously develop and reflect on your ability to demonstrate self-management skills, managing both the project and your state of mind.
  - Organization skills
  - Affective skills
  - Reflection skills.

Taking action

Taking action is where you apply your thinking, communication and social skills to creating your Personal Project product/ outcome. Make sure you consistently reflect and document your reflections in your process journal - make the process of creating visible.

Don't forget your global context! Take time to reflect on how your understanding of your chosen global context is deepening as a result of putting your investigating and planning into action.

Demonstrate your creative-thinking skills, critical-thinking skills and transfer-thinking skills. You can employ the various visible thinking routines in this chapter to help you communicate your thinking skills.

Demonstrate your communication and social skills. Questions and guidelines in this chapter can help you articulate how you have demonstrated your communication and social skills.

CHAPTER 5

Taking action

Create a product/outcome in response to the goal, global context and criteria

This chapter will guide you through the critical- and creative-thinking skills, transfer skills and communication and social skills required for putting your investigating and planning into action. Remember, the personal project inquiry cycle is iterative and interactive in its nature; as you take action you will most likely also need to engage in research, adjust your planning and employ affective skills such as overcoming obstacles through resilience and learning to bounce back.

ATL skills

- Organization skills
- Critical-thinking skills
- Creative-thinking skills
- Transfer skills

LEARNER PROFILE ATTRIBUTES

Thinkers

Communicators

Risk-takers

Your focus on the process of putting your personal project goal into action is an essential part of your personal project as a whole. Make sure you make the process of taking action visible through documenting the journey in your process journal. Although you are creating a product/outcome that you are very proud of, it is the learning acquired throughout this process that is of utmost and enduring importance.

Drawing together your investigating and planning you now need to put this into action and actually create your personal project product/outcome.

Enjoy the process, create prototypes, try multiple approaches to achieving your goal and simply immerse yourself in the creation process.

Your process journal should by now be becoming quite full with all your thinking made visible. Within this part of the personal project inquiry cycle, your process journal should be filled with photographs, screenshots, reflections, annotations, musings and everything that captures the process of creating your product/outcome.

EXPERT TIP

Make sure you consistently refer back to your criteria for success and your means of planning as you work towards accomplishing your personal project goal. No doubt you will come across hiccups in the process of taking action, never fear, this is all part of the process. Make sure you reflect on how you have adjusted the planning process within the given time frame and in your process journal justify why you have made these adjustments.

■ GLOBAL CONTEXT REMINDER

Remember to make sure that your chosen global context is not forgotten. Choose strategic points throughout the taking action process to pause, reflect and self-assess by asking yourself the following question:

- How is my product/outcome reflecting the global context I have chosen?

Communicate with a friend, family member, peer, mentor, supervisor or a person or group of people of your choosing to receive meaningful feedback by asking the following questions:

- Is the chosen global context evident in my product/outcome?
- From viewing my work, can you develop a different or deeper understanding of the global context I have chosen?

Take the feedback on board, ensure this is documented in your process journal and make necessary adjustments to ensure that your product/outcome is truly in response to the global context you have chosen.

You will find as you take action, you will need to engage in further research, adjust your planning and rethink aspects of your project – this is fine, the personal project is iterative and interactive, we move from element to element and back again throughout all significant and worthwhile projects. This way of thinking is what helps us grow as flexible and open-minded learners.

Demonstrate thinking skills

This part of the personal project inquiry cycle is embedded throughout each step of the project.

As you place into action your personal project goal you need to make your thinking visible in your process journal. Ensure you reflect continuously and show how you are developing your critical-, creative- and transfer-thinking skills.

In your process journal provide examples with explanations of how you have demonstrated thinking skills as you have developed your personal project product/outcome.

ACTIVITY: UNDERSTANDING YOUR TOPIC OR PRODUCT

ATL skills

- Critical-thinking skills
  - Practise observing carefully in order to recognize problems
  - Revise understanding based on new information and evidence

How is your understanding of the topic of your product/outcome developing?

To explain and provide evidence of how your understanding of the chosen topic of your product/outcome is developing you can employ the visible thinking routine *Claim – Support – Question.*

This routine enables you to explain clearly what you have learnt, provide evidence and continue the inquiry and action process through asking further questions.

Make a claim about the topic of your product/outcome that you have been exploring. A claim is an explanation or interpretation of some aspect of what is being examined.

Identify support or evidence for your claim. What do you now know? How can you provide evidence to support this claim?

Raise a question related to your claim. What may make you doubt the claim? What seems left hanging? What isn't fully explained? What further ideas or issues does your claim raise?

ACTIVITY: PROBLEM SOLVING

ATL skills

- Critical-thinking skills
  - Practise observing carefully in order to recognize problems
  - Propose and evaluate a variety of solutions
- Creative-thinking skills
  - Create novel solutions to authentic problems

What obstacles have you encountered?

As you progress through the process of creating your product/outcome, record in your process journal obstacles that you encounter. Putting a goal and plan into action comes with its challenges, so be sure to think carefully about how you can overcome these obstacles.

How have you overcome obstacles through problem solving?

Describe and explain how you have overcome the obstacles you have encountered in the taking action process. Take photographs, screenshots, recordings, sketches and so on to make your problem-solving skills visible.

ACTIVITY: NEW IDEAS AND PERSPECTIVES

ATL skills

- Critical-thinking skills
  - Analyse complex concepts and projects into their constituent parts and synthesize them to create new understanding
- Creative-thinking skills
  - Consider multiple alternatives, including those that might be unlikely or impossible
- Transfer skills
  - Apply skills and knowledge in unfamiliar situations
  - Transfer current knowledge to learning of new technologies

How have you generated novel ideas and considered new perspectives? How have you made connections between what you already knew to what you are learning in the process of taking action?

Generating novel ideas often comes as a result of exploring others' ideas, thinking deeply and challenging our own ideas, and building on from these ideas as a result of challenging our own thinking. A visible thinking routine that you can employ is *Connect – Extend – Challenge.*

As you engage in the process of taking action and putting into practice ideas and skills acquired through investigating and planning, ask yourself the following questions:

- How are the ideas and information connected to what I already knew?
- What new ideas did I get that extended or broadened my thinking in new directions?
- What challenges or puzzles have arisen from the ideas and information presented?

ACTIVITY: FEEDBACK

ATL skills

- Critical-thinking skills
  - Revise understanding based on new information and evidence
  - Propose and evaluate a variety of solutions
- Creative-thinking skills
  - Practise flexible thinking – develop multiple opposing, contradictory and complementary arguments
- Transfer skills
  - Combine knowledge, understanding and skills to create products or solutions

How have you taken feedback on board and incorporated this into the creation of your product/outcome?

Giving and receiving feedback is an important skill throughout the process of taking action. The quality of the feedback given and received can determine the overall quality of your product/outcome. The skill of giving and receiving feedback often lies in the questions we ask in order to dig deeper and broaden the scope of feedback. A concise visible thinking routine that you can employ is the *What Makes You Say That? (WMYST?)* routine.

As you receive feedback, dig deeper by asking the question *WMYST?* as many times as necessary in order to gather the best possible depth of feedback. In turn, as you give feedback, share this visible thinking routine with the person or group of people you are giving feedback to in order for them to receive from you the best possible depth of feedback.

ACTIVITY: FLEXIBLE THINKING SKILLS

ATL skills

- Critical-thinking skills
  - Consider ideas from multiple perspectives
  - Analyse complex concepts and projects into their constituent parts and synthesize them to create new understanding
- Creative-thinking skills
  - Make unexpected or unusual connections between objects and/or ideas
  - Practise flexible thinking – develop multiple opposing, contradictory and complementary arguments
  - Practise visible thinking strategies and techniques
- Transfer skills
  - Combine knowledge, understanding and skills to create products or solutions

How have you developed flexible thinking strategies surrounding the ethical impact of your product/outcome?

Using the following visible thinking routine, *Circle of viewpoints,* develop your flexible thinking strategies to consider the ethical impact of your product/outcome.

- *I am thinking of* [your product/outcome] *from the point of view of …*
- *I think …* [describe the ethical impact of your product/outcome from your chosen viewpoint. Be an actor – take on the character of your viewpoint]. *Because …* [explain your reasoning]
- *A question/concern I have from this viewpoint is …*

ACTIVITY: USING YOUR PRIOR KNOWLEDGE

ATL skills

- Critical-thinking skills
  - Revise understanding based on new information and evidence
- Creative-thinking skills
  - Make unexpected or unusual connections between objects and/or ideas
- Transfer skills
  - Apply skills and knowledge in unfamiliar situations
  - Combine knowledge, understanding and skills to create products or solutions

How have you employed your prior learning in the creation of your product/outcome?

Scroll or flick through your process journal to find where you have outlined the prior learning that will be employed to create the product/outcome. Provide evidence and explain how you have employed this prior learning effectively to create your product/outcome.

How you have used your subject-specific knowledge and skills in multiple contexts?

Scroll or flick through your process journal to find where you have outlined the subject-specific knowledge that will be employed to create the product/outcome. Provide evidence and explain how you have employed this subject-specific knowledge effectively to create your product/outcome.

ACTIVITY: GLOBAL CONTEXT INSIGHT

ATL skills

- Critical-thinking skills
  - Revise understanding based on new information and evidence
- Creative-thinking skills
  - Consider multiple alternatives, including those that might be unlikely or impossible
  - Make unexpected or unusual connections between objects and/or ideas
- Transfer skills
  - Combine knowledge, understanding and skills to create products or solutions

What new insight do you have into your chosen global context?

Using the following thinking routine, *I used to think, but now I think,* reflect on how your thinking has changed as a result of new insights into your chosen global context.

Use these sentence starters to explain your deeper insight into your chosen global context:

- *I used to think … but now I think … and this is why …*

The global contexts are very broad and complex for your project. Another way of explaining new insights into your chosen global context is through creating an *iceberg structure* to show depth of understanding.

Draw an iceberg structure (as pictured below) and at the top of the iceberg, the part above water, jot down what you notice and what is obvious about the global context you have chosen through the lens of your product/outcome. In the larger part under the water, dive deeper to examine the less obvious and explain the influences, values, beliefs and reasons for what you notice or what is obvious in the top part of the iceberg.

Make sure your responses to these questions are documented throughout your process journal. You may choose to spend some time responding to these questions or your own questions at one point in the project, or you may find that simply responding as you go works best for you. Draw pictures, jot down inspirational quotes, create diagrams, glue in printed images and articles – make your thinking as visible as possible.

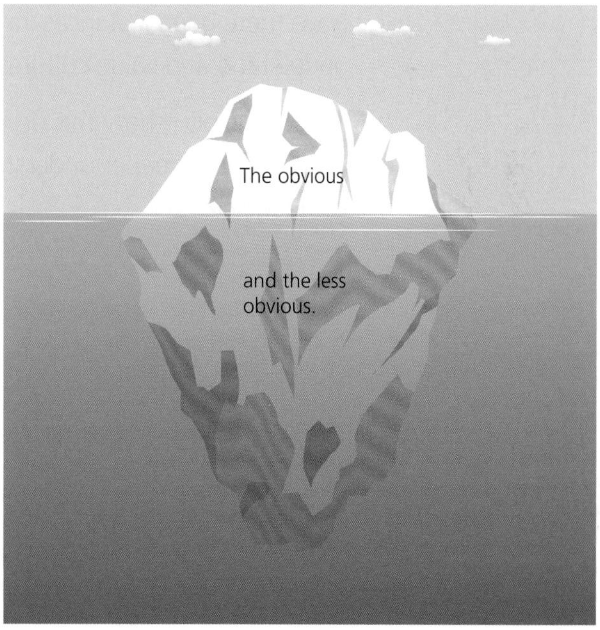
The obvious
and the less obvious.

Demonstrate communication and social skills

This part of the personal project inquiry cycle is embedded throughout each step of the project. As you place into action your personal project goal you will be growing as a communicator by developing your communication and social skills. Ensure you reflect continuously and show how you are developing as a collaborative learner and as a communicator.

How have you developed a deeper sense of empathy?

Through overcoming obstacles and solving problems, can you explain how you can understand and share the feelings that others have experienced when they have had to overcome obstacles and solve problems?

How have you developed intercultural understanding?

Have there been instances in your personal project journey where you have learnt to understand and value cultures, belief systems and languages other than your own?

Can you explain how this development of intercultural understanding has enabled you to have a deeper understanding of your own culture(s), belief systems and language(s)?

ACTIVITY: RESOLVING CONFLICT

ATL skills

- Communication skills
  - Give and receive meaningful feedback
  - Negotiate ideas and knowledge with peers and teachers
- Collaboration skills
  - Take responsibility for one's own actions
  - Listen actively to other perspectives and ideas
  - Encourage others to contribute

How have you managed to resolve conflict and work collaboratively with others?

Throughout sustained projects that require collaboration and communication skills, conflicts can arise and create a need for employing conflict resolution skills. An approach to effective conflict resolution that you are no doubt familiar with as IB students is through creating essential agreements.

When creating an essential agreement with the person or group of people you are collaborating with, it is beneficial to use the following steps as a guide:

1. Realign yourselves with the purpose: What is it that you are creating? What is the purpose?
2. Consider what helps you and the person or group of people you are collaborating with to best produce the work required. Think about the environment, physical structures and preferred learning styles.
3. Discuss what this looks like, sounds like and feels like. You can create a Y-Chart to record your discussion.
4. Using the information from this discussion, create *We will ...* statements. For example, *We will listen actively to one another and wait until the other person has finished sharing their ideas before responding.*
5. As you progress in the collaborative process, refer to your essential agreement should conflict arise and you need a reminder of the agreed upon approaches to collaboration and communication.

How have you taken responsibility for your actions?

Reflect on the process of taking action and creating your product/outcome. Where have you had to take responsibility for your actions? Perhaps you overspent your budget, or struggled to manage your time effectively and needed to reassess how you will go further or perhaps something has broken in the process of taking action? Reflect on how you have been a principled learner who has owned what has happened rather than blaming skills you have, and how by employing your self-management skills you have moved forward.

How have you encouraged others to contribute to your personal project? How have you worked effectively with members of the community who are your mentors throughout this project? How have you worked effectively with your supervisor and taken their ideas on board?

Think of how you have engaged with your mentor and experts in the field of the topic you have chosen, members of your community and your Personal Project supervisor. How have you encouraged them to contribute to your personal project? How have you sought meaningful feedback from others as a means of them contributing to your personal project?

How have you exercised leadership?

As a personal project student you have leadership over your personal project journey that requires coordination, collaboration and communication with others. Exercising leadership requires a clear goal and communication and negotiation skills. How have you communicated the needs of your project through exercising leadership to help you achieve your personal project goal? Reflect on how your leadership skills have developed and how these developing skills will support you in further studies and project management.

ACTIVITY: GIVING AND RECEIVING FEEDBACK

ATL skills

- Communication skills
  - Give and receive meaningful feedback
  - Make inferences and draw conclusions
- Collaboration skills
  - Listen actively to other perspectives and ideas
  - Encourage others to contribute
  - Give and receive meaningful feedback

How have you given and received meaningful feedback?

If you have employed the visible thinking routine *What Makes You Say That? (WMYST?)* or a similar approach, how have you further developed your skills for giving and receiving meaningful feedback? Another means of giving and receiving meaningful feedback is through employing the *Ladder of feedback*.

1 Begin at the first rung of the ladder and begin by offering or receiving meaningful feedback through **clarification** of your product/outcome. You can ask and encourage others to ask you the following questions:
   - I wasn't sure about?
   - Could you help me better understand?

2 Follow this by climbing to the second rung (figuratively) discussing the **value** of your product/outcome. You can use the following sentence starters as a guide:
   - What I like is …
   - One opposite point is …

3 Then move to the third rung and express **concerns** surrounding your product/outcome. You can use the following sentence starters as a guide:
   - Have you considered …
   - What I wonder about is …
   - Perhaps you have thought about this, but …

4 Moving to the final rung of the feedback ladder you can offer **suggestions** and seek suggestions from others. The following sentence starter can be employed as a guide:
   - Can I suggest that …

How have you organized and depicted information logically?

Take some time to reflect on how you are presenting your record of your development through your personal project journey in your process journal. It is a good idea to highlight sections of your personal project journey according to the personal project objectives. For example, when you are problem solving by employing your critical- and creative-thinking skills, highlight in your process journal how this is you demonstrating your ATL thinking skills. This organization and logical depiction of information will help others understand your personal project journey and also provide support at the end of this project when you are writing your personal project report and piecing together your appendices.

Make sure your responses to the questions above that you believe are relevant to your process of taking action, are documented throughout your process journal. You may choose to spend some time responding to these questions or your own questions at one point in the project, or you may find that simply responding as you go works best for you.

EXPERT TIP

Take notes from interviews, jot down minutes from meetings, create diagrams, use emojis to express emotions that come from collaboration and communication and so on to make sure your communication and social skills are visible. Using multiple technology platforms can help you on your journey of demonstrating your communication and social skills; rather than taking notes you could record or film your social interactions or use an online survey platform to conduct surveys and analyse the data gathered. Take risks using new media and see which media platforms you can transfer to other areas of study and project management.

Supervisor check-in

- Share your challenges and how you have overcome these challenges by employing your thinking skills in the process of creating your product/outcome.
- With each supervisor check-in, make sure you record the key points from your meeting and reflect on how you have taken their feedback on board.
- Share how you have demonstrated your communication and social skills through the process of creating your product/outcome. Seek feedback from your supervisor about how you can improve your communication and social skills.

CHAPTER SUMMARY KEY POINTS

- Taking action is where you apply your thinking, communication and social skills to creating your personal project product/outcome. Make sure you consistently reflect and document your reflections in your process journal – make the process of creating visible.
- Don't forget your global context! Take time to reflect on how your understanding of your chosen global context is deepening as a result of putting your investigating and planning into action.
- Demonstrate your creative-thinking skills, critical-thinking skills and transfer skills. You can employ the various visible thinking routines in this chapter to help you communicate your thinking skills.
- Demonstrate your communication and social skills. Questions and guidelines in this chapter can help you articulate how you have demonstrated your communication and social skills.

Reflecting

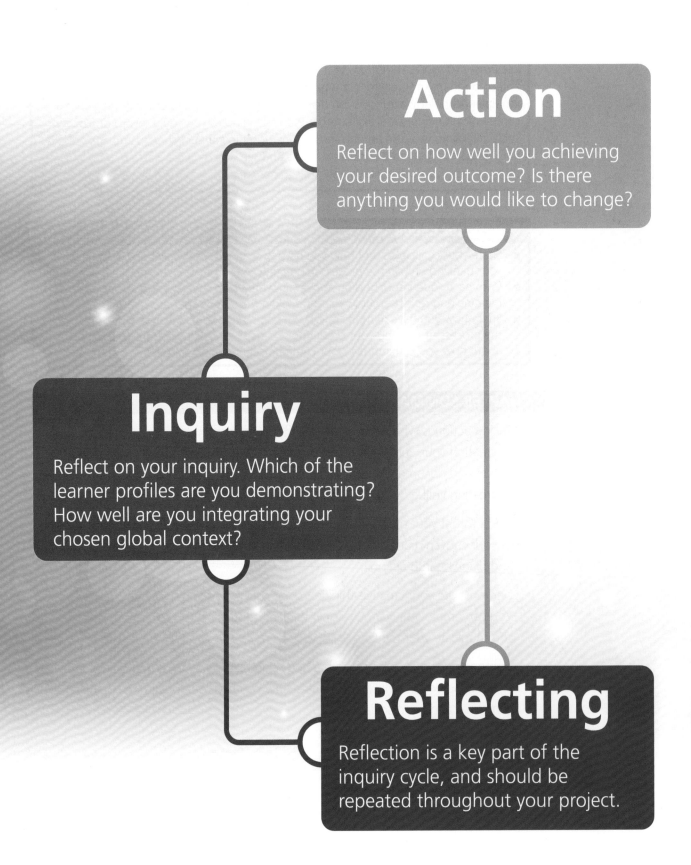

Action

Reflect on how well you achieving your desired outcome? Is there anything you would like to change?

Inquiry

Reflect on your inquiry. Which of the learner profiles are you demonstrating? How well are you integrating your chosen global context?

Reflecting

Reflection is a key part of the inquiry cycle, and should be repeated throughout your project.

CHAPTER 6

Reflecting

Evaluating and reflecting: The importance of reflection

ATL skills

- Collaboration skills
- Affective skills
- Reflection skills
- Transfer skills

LEARNER PROFILE ATTRIBUTES

Communicators

Reflective

Reflection is not something that happens just at the end of the project; it is part of the whole process. Indeed, reflection is a key component of the inquiry cycle, and this cycle can – and should – be repeated multiple times throughout the project. It is only through engaging in multiple, iterative cycles of inquiry that you will be able to demonstrate the highest levels of achievement.

EXPERT TIP

Reflection is not a linear process, so you will likely reflect on the three strands of Criterion D at different stages throughout your project. Therefore, it is important to reflect regularly in your process journal – not just in the report – on the areas addressed below. Your report will simply pull all of these reflections together at the end.

Evaluating the quality of the product/outcome against your criteria

The first strand of Criterion D considers how you evaluate the quality of your product or outcome against the criteria you set for yourself in the beginning stages of your project. In order to reach the top mark band, you will have to evaluate the product or outcome against all of the criteria; identifying the strengths, weaknesses and possible improvements you could have made to the product/outcome.

ACTIVITY: REFLECTING ON YOUR SPECIFICATIONS

ATL skills

- Reflection skills
  - Identify strengths and weaknesses of personal learning strategies (self-assessment)
- Transfer skills
  - Combine knowledge, understanding and skills to create products or solutions

Think back to the criteria, or specifications, you created during the planning stage of your project. In what ways can you measure the success of your product against each of these criteria? To do this, you may want to make a list of *qualitative* versus *quantifiable* criteria. (See Chapter 4.)

	Specification 1	Specification 2	Specification 3	Specification 4
Excellent				
Substantial				
Adequate				
Limited				

Reflecting on how completing the project has extended your knowledge and understanding of the topic and the global context

By now, you will have no doubt acquired a great deal more knowledge about your chosen topic than you had at the beginning of the project. It is important to reflect on what, specifically, you have learnt. Did you learn more about a particular subject? Or did you learn a new skill – or develop an existing skill? Your report should include specific examples of how completing the project has extended your knowledge and understanding of your topic.

ACTIVITY: KNOW–WANT TO KNOW–LEARNT

ATL skills

- Reflection skills
  - Consider content
- Transfer skills
  - Make connections between subject groups and disciplines

In Chapter 3, you considered what you already knew about your chosen topic as well as what you wanted to learn through the process of inquiry. Now reflect on what you have actually learnt by completing the final column of the KWL chart.

K: What do you already KNOW about your chosen topic?

W: What do you WANT to learn through your process of inquiry?

L: What have you LEARNT? What knowledge have you gained or skills have you developed?

K	W	L

You should also have developed a greater understanding of your chosen global context. If you remember from Chapter 3, the global context should serve as the lens through which you focus your inquiry; therefore, the global context should have shaped the way you approached your project.

ACTIVITY: GROUP DISCUSSION

ATL skills

- Collaboration skills
  - Listen actively to other perspectives and ideas
  - Give and receive meaningful feedback

Form a group with three to four other students. Ideally, each of these students should have focused their project on a different global context; however, even if you focused on the same global context as someone else, you will likely have approached the process differently. Refer to the global context table on page 31 to help you.

Discuss the following questions:

1 Why did you initially choose your global context?
2 In what ways did your global context shape your inquiry?
3 How might using a different global context have changed your inquiry or the end product?
4 What new understandings have you developed of your chosen global context?

Reflecting on your development as an IB learner through the project

Completing the personal project is a significant milestone in your MYP journey. Throughout the experience, you will have drawn on much of the knowledge you have gained and many of the skills you have developed throughout your MYP studies. It is now time to reflect on how you have developed as an IB learner; we do this through the lens of the learner profile.

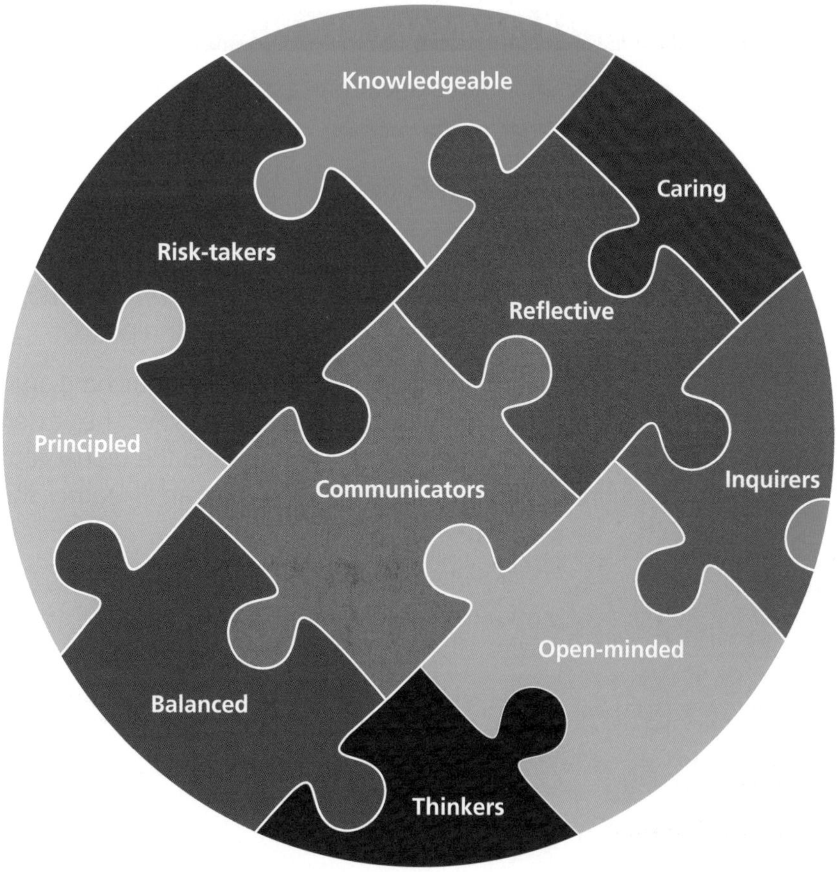
Knowledgeable
Caring
Risk-takers
Reflective
Principled
Communicators
Inquirers
Open-minded
Balanced
Thinkers

ACTIVITY: REFLECTING ON THE LEARNER PROFILES

ATL skills

- Affective skills
  - Resilience – practise "bouncing back" after adversity, mistakes and failures; practise dealing with disappointment and unmet expectations
- Reflection skills
  - Identify strengths and weaknesses of personal learning strategies (self-assessment)
  - Consider ATL skills development

Think–Pair–Share

Think about the questions below, then discuss them with a partner before sharing with the rest of the class.

1. How have you developed as an IB learner (using the learner profile)? What qualities do you think you have demonstrated, and how?
2. Consider the strengths and weaknesses you have displayed in completing your project.
3. What specific challenges did you face, and how did you overcome those challenges?
4. What impact do you think this project could have on your future learning?

Supervisor check-in

- Share your reflections with your supervisor during your meetings. Among other questions, you could consider the following:
  - ☐ What new insights have you gained into your chosen topic or global context?
  - ☐ What challenges have you faced that you didn't anticipate? How did you overcome those challenges?
  - ☐ What skills have you developed?
  - ☐ How have you grown as a learner?

CHAPTER SUMMARY KEY POINTS

- Reflection is not a linear process. It is part of the inquiry cycle and will form part of all stages of the project.
- You should show evidence of ongoing reflection within your process journal and report.
- There are three specific aspects of reflection which you will need to explicitly address in the Reflecting section of your report:
  - evaluating the quality of the product/outcome against your criteria
  - reflecting on how completing the project has extended your knowledge and understanding of the topic and the global context
  - reflecting on your development as an IB learner through the project.

Reporting the Personal Project

Format

- The project report is distinct from the product. The project report is a formal reflection on the process.
- You have a choice of four possible formats for the report: written, electronic, oral, or visual.

Structure

- The report must be structured around the assessment criteria.

Academic honesty

- Academic honesty must be practised throughout the process, and all sources must be acknowledged according to recognised conventions.
- You will be required to submit an academic honesty form to the IB as part of the moderation process. This form will need to be signed by your supervisor to authenticate your work.

Appendix

- You will need to include up to 10 A4 pages of process journal entries in the appendix of your report.

CHAPTER 7

Reporting the Personal Project

ATL skills

- Communication skills
- Collaboration skills
- Organization skills
- Reflection skills
- Information literacy skills

LEARNER PROFILE ATTRIBUTES

Knowledgeable

Communicators

Principled

Reflective

The final stage of the personal project is to report on your process. It is important to note, as mentioned in Chapter 3, that the report is distinct from the product. Even if you have produced a report as the end product of your goal, you must still produce a reflective report which evaluates your process and addresses each of the assessment criteria.

Possible formats of the report

You have a choice of four different report formats to suit your own learning style. Oral, visual and multimedia reports must be recorded for internal standardization purposes and for possible submission to the IB for moderation.

Format	Length		
	English, French, Spanish and Arabic	**Chinese**	**Japanese**
Written	1,500–3,500 words	1,800–4,200 characters	3,000–7,000 kana/kanji
Electronic (website, blog, slideshow)	1,500–3,500 words	1,800–4,200 characters	3,000–7,000 kana/kanji
Oral (podcast, radio broadcast, recorded)	13–15 minutes	13–15 minutes	13–15 minutes
Visual (film)	13–15 minutes	13–15 minutes	13–15 minutes

EXPERT TIP

If you fully engage with the process journal and use it effectively as a tool for documenting the planning and development of your project, then you should be able to use much of the same material within your report. You may need to reword it slightly to suit the academic register expected of a formal report, but you should have a lot of ideas to work with.

Using the assessment criteria

Whatever format of report you choose, you must address each strand of the assessment criteria. Think of the assessment criteria as your skeletal outline. The criteria can serve as your section headings, and the individual strands are the points or topics you will develop in further detail within each section.

Tips for completing a written report

- Use the assessment criteria to structure your report. A written report should have identifiable sections which align with each of the criteria. You may also wish to label each sub-section according to the different strands of the criteria.
- The personal project report is a *reflective* report. Therefore, your voice should come through loud and clear. This may be a new style of writing for you as many subject teachers advise a more objective voice; some teachers may have explicitly told you not to use first person in your essays. In the personal project report, you should be actively reflecting on your own experiences as an IB learner.
- Make sure you format your report using standard conventions such as font size, spacing, page size and orientation, page numbers and so on. Your school may have a "house style" they expect you to follow. If in doubt, ask your supervisor or Personal Project Coordinator.
- Where appropriate, make reference to process journal entries which may provide further evidence of each of the criteria.
- Cite any material which is not your own in both the body of your report and in the bibliography.
- Use a recognized referencing system for citing your sources. (There is more on this later in the chapter.)
- Proofread – more than once – for errors in spelling, grammar and sentence structure. While your use of language is not directly assessed, your ability to communicate clearly and coherently is assessed within Criterion C ("demonstrate communication and social skills"). If your language impedes the reader's/examiner's ability to understand your ideas, this may indirectly impact your mark.

Tips for delivering an oral report

- Use the assessment criteria to structure your report.
- Less is more when it comes to visuals. Don't overload your slides with text; your audience likely won't take the time to read it. Remember that *you* are the presentation; any accompanying slides that you prepare should serve as an aid, not a distraction.
- By all means, use note cards as prompts during the presentation, but do not read directly from them. Nothing turns an audience off more than a presenter who is unengaging.
- As above, remember to engage with your audience. Make eye contact, be aware of any nervous tics you may have (for example, pacing back and forth or nail biting). Talk *to* the audience, not *at* them. For inspiration, watch some TED Talks to see how the professionals do it.
- Take it slow. You have up to 15 minutes, so don't rush through the material. Speak clearly and coherently. Remember that part of Criterion C assesses your ability to demonstrate communication and social skills.
- Acknowledge any sources that you refer to in your report. This would be the equivalent of in-text citation for a written report.
- Practise, practise, practise. Perform your oral report for a friend, family member or in front of a mirror before you deliver it live. Remember, you only have one opportunity to deliver your report, so the more prepared you are, the better.

EXPERT TIP

You might start writing your report before you have fully completed your project. If this is the case, it is important to remember to write in the past tense. Your process journal is a place to record the development of your project, which includes more immediate, "in-the-moment" reflection, but the report is a reflection on the entire process.

ACTIVITY: PLANNING YOUR ORAL REPORT

ATL skills

- Organization skills
  - Create plans to prepare for summative assessments (examinations and performances)

Complete a storyboard or visual plan for an oral report. In the boxes, you could sketch or list in bullet points what to include in the visual element of your report (for example, PowerPoint, Google Slides or Prezi). The lines underneath allow space for you to write out a brief script of what you intend to say that may not be included in the visual component.

Note: An annotated example of a written report is included in the appendices.

Academic honesty

Academic honesty involves producing work which is original and, where relevant, acknowledging the work of others who have influenced your own work. Academic honesty is a guiding principle of all academic institutions and organizations, including the IB. The philosophy of academic honesty aligns very closely with the learner profile. As *principled* learners, "we act with integrity and honesty, with a strong sense of fairness and justice, and with respect for the dignity and rights of people everywhere. We take responsibility for our actions and their consequences."

There are many forms of academic *dis*honesty, but due to the nature of the personal project, those which are most applicable in this context are plagiarism, collusion and fabrication.

Plagiarism: Plagiarism is using work from another source without acknowledging that source. Plagiarism may be deliberate or unintentional; either way, it is still considered "stealing". Any ideas which are not your own must be cited.

Collusion: Collusion is when two or more students work together on an assignment which is meant to be independent. This is different from collaboration, which is an important aspect of the approaches to learning. Collusion is a deliberate act and might involve copying from a classmate.

Fabrication: Fabrication includes inventing or misrepresenting information. This could include making up data in the experimental sciences, using fictional case studies (presented as real-life case studies) in the human sciences, or reflecting on experiences which did not happen to you.

Academic misconduct could have far-reaching consequences and future implications on your academic career. If you are caught practising academic dishonesty in the IB Diploma Programme, you could risk losing your Diploma. At university level, you could potentially face expulsion. Outside of the academic world there have been several high-profile cases of plagiarism which have led to legal proceedings. Even claims which are not proven have tarnished reputations. Singer-songwriter Bob Dylan was hit with plagiarism claims when it was suggested by writer Ben Greenman that a quote Dylan referenced in his 2016 Nobel Prize acceptance speech was lifted from SparkNotes.

EXPERT TIP

Many schools now use plagiarism-checking websites such as TurnItIn to check for originality. The IB also uses plagiarism-checking software. It is not worth the risk to your academic reputation to turn in work which is not 100 per cent original or appropriately sourced. If in doubt, always cite!

EXPERT TIP

It is important to acknowledge that different cultures may have different attitudes towards academic honesty. Whatever your own personal views on academic honesty may be, you must follow the guidelines set out by the IB. As such, you will be expected to submit an academic honesty form, signed by your supervisor, as part of the moderation process (discussed in more detail in Chapter 10).

A note about word limits

The IB has strict guidelines regarding word limits. External moderators for the IB are instructed not to read beyond 3,500 words, so it is important that you adhere to these guidelines. If your report is above the maximum word limit, you will be penalized.

Included in the 3,500 word count	Not included in the 3,500 word count
All main sections of the report, including section headings	The title page
Quotations	Table of contents
Footnotes not used for referencing	Maps, charts, diagrams, annotated illustrations, data tables, or other figures
Endnotes not used for referencing	Internal citations and references (including footnotes used for referencing)
	The bibliography
	Appendices and process journal extracts

EXPERT TIP

You are required to include a word count on the title page of your report. Be accurate; this is part of academic honesty. Since all personal projects are uploaded digitally to the IB for moderation, it is easy for the moderators to verify the word count if they suspect it falls outside of the guidelines.

Citation and referencing

As with any other piece of academic coursework you complete, you must cite any sources that you have consulted, whether directly or paraphrased.

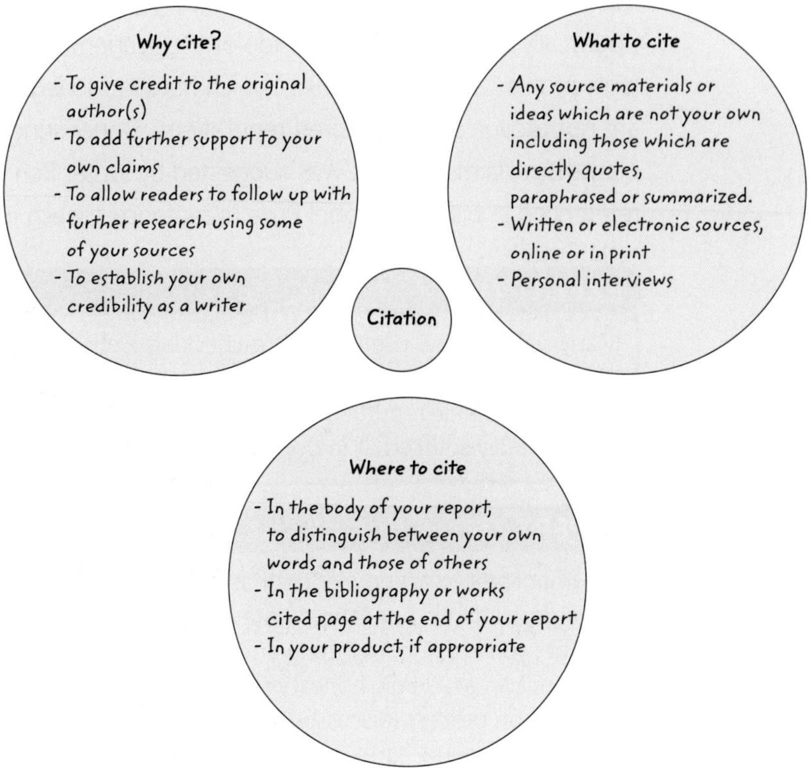
Why cite?
- To give credit to the original author(s)
- To add further support to your own claims
- To allow readers to follow up with further research using some of your sources
- To establish your own credibility as a writer
What to cite
- Any source materials or ideas which are not your own including those which are directly quotes, paraphrased or summarized.
- Written or electronic sources, online or in print
- Personal interviews
Citation
Where to cite
- In the body of your report, to distinguish between your own words and those of others
- In the bibliography or works cited page at the end of your report
- In your product, if appropriate

The IB does not stipulate which referencing style you use. This is up to your school. Whatever style your school expects from you (APA, Chicago, Harvard, MLA and so on), you must be consistent. There are many free websites, such as EasyBib or Citethisforme, which will help you create a bibliography that is formatted according to the referencing style your school expects.

EXPERT TIP

You will likely consult multiple sources throughout the research process. It is a good idea to keep a set of note cards or a digital file for each source that you consult, whether or not you end up using that information in your final product or report. Organizing your information in this way will make it easier to cite your sources in your final report; your files can also serve as a running bibliography.

EXPERT TIP

There is a difference between a bibliography and a works cited page. A bibliography consists of all of the sources you have consulted throughout the process. A works cited includes only those sources which are directly cited in your report or product. Your Personal Project Coordinator or supervisor should be able to advise you on which format is more appropriate to your project.

Further guidance on academic honesty, citation and referencing

There are several resources available online to give you further information on academic honesty, including:

Academic Honesty in the IB educational context: **http://www.ibo.org/globalassets/digital-tookit/brochures/academic-honesty-ib-en.pdf**

Effective citing and referencing: **http://www.ibo.org/globalassets/digital-tookit/brochures/effective-citing-and-referencing-en.pdf**

You can also view the winning film from the IB's 2016 Academic honesty film competition (MYP), available on the IB Community Blog: **http://blogs.ibo.org/blog/2017/05/26/myp-winners-academic-honesty-film-competition/**

Selecting the appendix

The final section of your report is the appendix. The appendix should consist of a selection of process journal entries. You are allowed to include up to ten A4 pages. It is a good idea to include entries from different stages of the project to sufficiently demonstrate the planning and development of your project, in line with Criterion B. The entries you select should ideally demonstrate a range of ATL skills and learner profile attributes. It would be a good idea to label each entry with these skills and attributes, as noted in Chapter 3, to signpost your ongoing reflection and self-evaluation to the examiner.

If your report is an oral presentation, you will still need to submit a bibliography and process journal extracts. You may also include the visual aids you used, but they will count towards the ten A4 pages or (annotated) screenshots you can submit in the appendices. This guidance also applies to visual and multimedia reports.

Tips for selecting appropriate process journal entries

This section provides some tips from students who have already completed their personal project, on how they chose which sections of their process journal to use in their appendix.

Objective A: Investigating

I have included in my process journal my personal project goal using the 5W1H method to make sure I am clearly explaining the scope of what I wish to achieve through the personal project.

Using the global context lens template, I have clearly shown in my process journal how I have deeply thought about the possibilities of my personal project goal through each of the global contexts. I want to show that I have thought about how my goal can be suited for each of the global contexts and have relevance in multiple settings.

After I had thought about and discussed with my supervisor the prior learning and subject-specific knowledge that will support the development of my personal project, I have jotted these down in my process journal and made connections with how this prior learning and subject-specific knowledge will be transferred to my personal project goal. From here, I plan to create inquiry questions that will guide my research.

In order to make sure I am being academically honest and also critically thinking about the sources I have researched, I have made this visible in my process journal in order for my supervisor to be assured that I am being transparent in the research process, demonstrating how I am being a principled learner through striving for absolute academic honesty.

Objective B: Planning

I have included the specifications I began with in order to develop success criteria for my personal project. By including this in my process journal I had a continual reference point to ensure that I was seeking to reach the best possible outcome of my personal project goal.

My success criteria was an integral part of my process journal. As I took action and created my personal project goal I referred to this part of my process journal continuously to ensure that I was developing work that was consistent with my goal.

Second to my success criteria, the inclusion of the Gantt Chart was the most continuously accessed element of my process journal. As other assessments for my MYP subjects came in, I made sure that I organised my time around the plans I had set for personal project completion.

Reflection on my self-management skills was the most difficult as this required very open honesty. However, I included this in my process journal and when discussing this reflection with my supervisor and friends, I found I wasn't alone – others were providing very honest reflections on their self-management skills. This knowledge of not being alone greatly helped me progress through the personal project.

■ Objective C: Taking action

I chose to document the process of creating my product not just as a means of evidence, but also as a way to encourage myself as I went through the process of taking action. When I reflected on how far I had come I was encouraged to keep at it and keep moving forward as I had already accomplished so much

The inclusion of my thinking skills was important to include in my process journal as I had to make sure that this mental process was made visible. By making my thinking processes visible, I could look back on why I made the decisions I had made and also to show my supervisor how my thinking was improving throughout the project.

I included screenshots of interactions with my supervisor as a means of providing evidence of my social skills throughout the project. This also meant I could show that my interactions with those who supported me throughout the personal project were respectful and professional.

■ Objective D: Reflecting

When reflecting on the success of my product against the specifications I created, I was able to refer back to the success criteria in my process journal and then provide justifications for each of the decisions I made in the self-assessment process.

I included my reflection on the global context in my process journal continuously as I wanted my project to truly reflect the guiding question of the global context I chose. By pausing, reflecting and explaining my new thoughts on the global context I had chosen, my product was able to truly reflect the global context.

I know the key to all success in learning is knowledge of self as learner. By including my thoughts on how I have developed the characteristics of each of the learner profile attributes I was able to identify my strengths as a learner and also look at where I need to put effort into further developing these strengths.

A checklist for the project report

Section 1 – Objective A: Investigating		
Define a clear goal and global context for the project, based on personal interests	I give the precise meaning of the goal of my project;	☐
	I explain "what I wanted to achieve; when, where, how and why I wanted to achieve it."	☐
	I define the global context that applies best to my project and explain its connection.	☐
	I describe what makes my project personal: the experiences, interests and ideas that make it important to me.	☐
	If I made changes to my goal during the project, I explain the changes and why I made them.	☐
Identify prior learning and subject-specific knowledge relevant to the project	I identify what I already knew about this topic/project and the sources of my knowledge.	☐
	I identify what I learnt in MYP subject groups before the project started, and how this was helpful.	☐

Demonstrate research skills	I outline the research skills I had when I started the project.	☐
	I discuss the research skills I developed through the project.	☐
	I explain how I may have shared my research skills to help peers who needed more practice.	☐
Section 2 – Objective B: Planning		
Develop criteria for the product/outcome	I refer to the criteria I developed to evaluate the project product/outcome.	☐
	If I made changes to my criteria during the project, I explain the changes and why I made them.	☐
Plan and record the development process of the project	I provide evidence of my planning through timelines, milestones or other tools/strategies.	☐
	I present a record of how the project progressed from start to finish.	☐
Demonstrate self-management skills	I outline the self-management skills I had when I started the project.	☐
	I discuss the self-management skills I developed through the project.	☐
	I explain how I may have shared my self-management skills to help peers who needed more practice.	☐
Section 3 – Objective C: Taking action		
Create a product/outcome in response to the goal, global context and criteria	I discuss the product/outcome as the result of the process undertaken during the project.	☐
	I check that I have included evidence of my product to be submitted with my report.	☐
Demonstrate thinking skills	I outline the thinking skills I had when I started the project.	☐
	I discuss the thinking skills I developed through the project.	☐
	I explain how I may have shared my thinking skills to help peers who needed more practice.	☐
Demonstrate communication and social skills	I outline the communication and social skills I had when I started the project.	☐
	I discuss the communication and social skills I developed through the project.	☐
	I explain how I may have shared my communication and social skills to help peers who needed more practice.	☐
Section 4 – Objective D: Reflecting		
Evaluate the quality of the product/outcome against their criteria	I evaluate the product/outcome against the criteria I designed.	☐
	I identify the strengths, weaknesses and possible improvements of the product/outcome.	☐
Reflect on how completing the project has extended their knowledge and understanding of the topic and the global context	I identify challenges and the solutions I developed to meet them.	☐
	I demonstrate a deeper knowledge and understanding of my topic and my identified global context.	☐
	I base my reflection on evidence, including my process journal.	☐
Reflect on their development as IB learners through the project	I identify how I have developed as a learner (using the IB learner profile as appropriate).	☐
	I discuss my strengths and weaknesses in completing the project.	☐
	I summarize the impact the project could have on my future learning.	☐

ACTIVITY: PEER OR SELF-ASSESSMENT

ATL skills

- Communication skills
  - Use a variety of speaking techniques to communicate with a variety of audiences
- Collaboration skills
  - Give and receive meaningful feedback
- Reflection skills
  - Identify strengths and weaknesses of personal learning strategies (self-assessment)
- Information literacy skills
  - Understand and implement intellectual property rights
  - Create references and citations, use footnotes/endnotes and construct a bibliography according to recognized conventions

Exchange a preliminary draft of one of the sections of your report with a peer. If you have chosen to complete a report in a different format, you can give them a brief plan or talk through your ideas as a sort of "rehearsal" for the oral report.

Use the checklist to ensure that your peer has included all of the relevant points within that section. Give your peer constructive feedback on what works well and what needs further improvement. When giving your feedback, consider the following:

1 How well developed are the ideas?

2 Does the student provide sufficiently detailed examples to support each of the strands of the assessment criteria?

3 How clear and coherent is the writing?

You could also complete this as a self-assessment exercise. In this case, it would be a good idea to use the assessed exemplar in the appendix as a model of good writing. How does your version compare? Have you addressed each strand of the criteria with sufficient depth and examples?

Supervisor check-in

- Ask your supervisor for advice if you are unsure of the style of report to complete. Your supervisor may well be one of your teachers and might therefore have some further insight into your learning style.
- Share a running bibliography with your supervisor throughout the different stages of the project.
- Consult your supervisor on when and how to appropriately cite your sources.
- If appropriate, use your supervisor as a subject expert. Remember to give him or her credit!
- The IB allows your supervisor to give you feedback on one complete draft of the report. Use this opportunity to gain constructive feedback – and act according to your supervisor's suggestions. Remember: your supervisor is there to help and guide you towards success.

CHAPTER SUMMARY KEY POINTS

- The project report is distinct from the product. The project report is a formal reflection on the process.
- You have a choice of four possible formats for the report: written, electronic, oral or visual.
- The report must be structured around the assessment criteria.
- Academic honesty must be practised throughout the process, and all sources must be acknowledged according to recognized conventions.
- You will be required to submit an academic honesty form to the IB as part of the moderation process. This form will need to be signed by your supervisor to authenticate your work.
- You will need to include up to ten A4 pages of process journal entries in the appendix of your report.

The role of

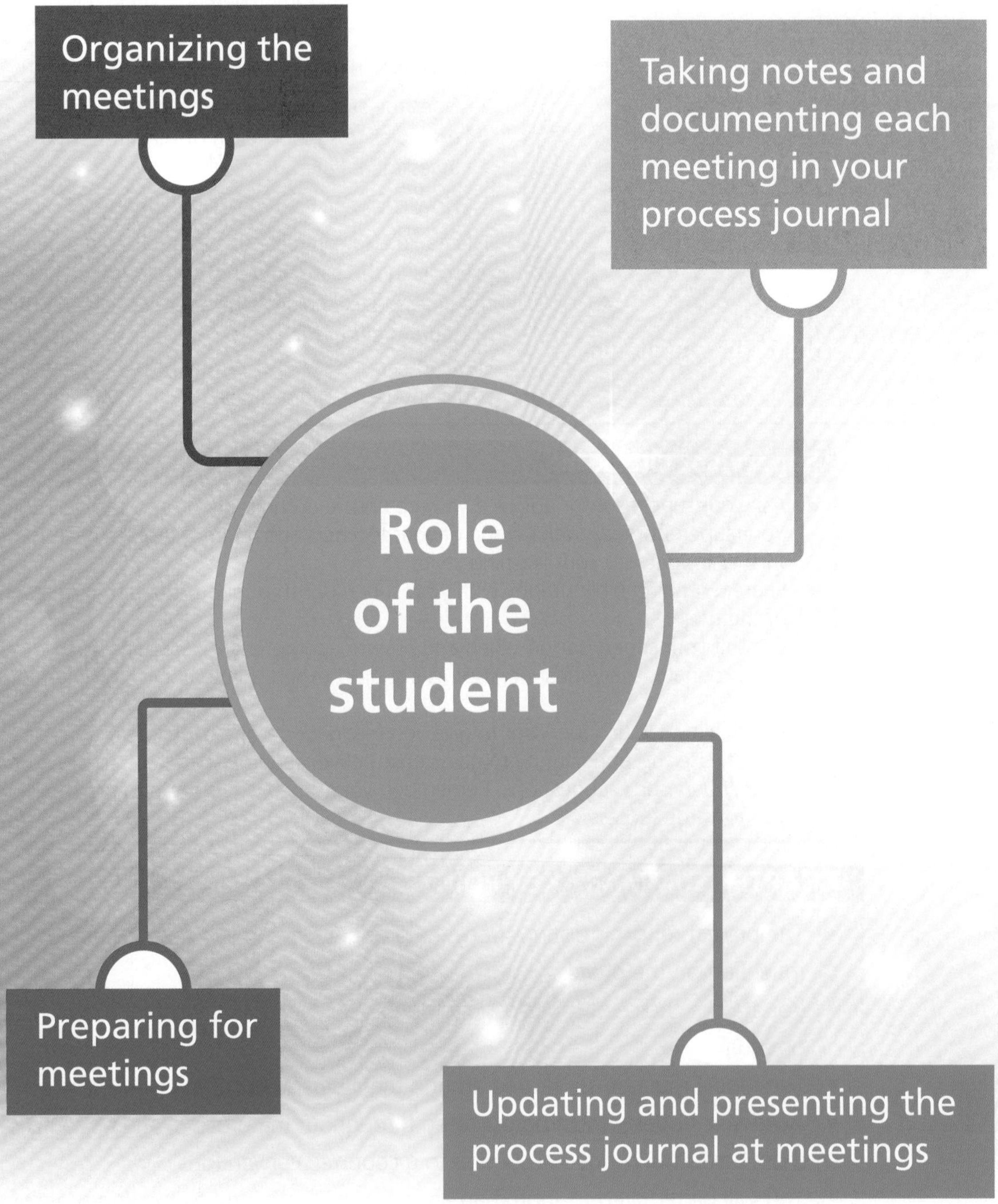
Organizing the meetings
Taking notes and documenting each meeting in your process journal
Role of the student
Preparing for meetings
Updating and presenting the process journal at meetings

the supervisor

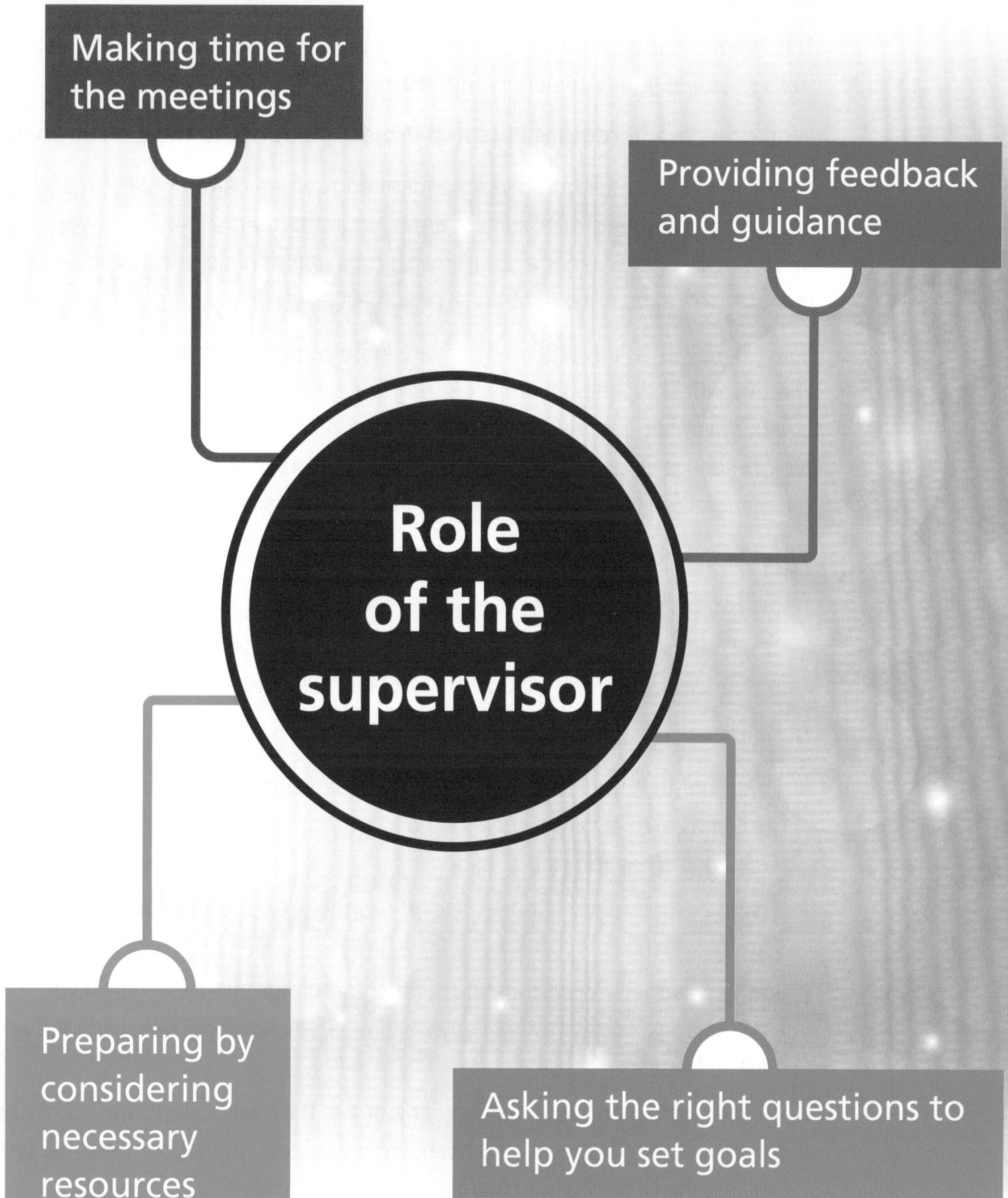
Making time for the meetings
Providing feedback and guidance
Role of the supervisor
Preparing by considering necessary resources
Asking the right questions to help you set goals

CHAPTER 8

The role of the supervisor

ATL skills

- Communication skills
- Collaboration skills

LEARNER PROFILE ATTRIBUTES		
Communicators	Open-minded	Balanced

This chapter outlines the "Why, What and How" of the role of your Personal Project supervisor and your interaction with them.

Why does the IB require Personal Project students to have a supervisor?

As the personal project is an independent and self-managed project that does not form part of your MYP subject areas, your allocated supervisor is your support person to help you manage the personal project independently and develop self-management skills outside of an MYP subject area classroom.

Support, collaboration and feedback are important for all projects, both at school and beyond. The personal project is a significant project that requires support, collaboration and feedback in order for you to experience the benefits of personal project engagement. Your supervisor is crucial as this support person is a key person to collaborate with and to provide you with timely, strategic and descriptive feedback.

What is the role of your Personal Project supervisor?

The Personal Project supervisor is primarily a support role, they are your one-person cheer squad so your personal project experience can be an experience that empowers you to flourish and grow as a self-managed learner.

The supervisor's responsibilities:

- To ensure that the topic you have chosen satisfies appropriate legal and ethical standards with regard to health and safety, confidentiality, human rights, animal welfare and environmental issues.
- To provide guidance and feedback throughout each part of the personal project inquiry cycle.
- In the personal project meetings that you organize, they will coach you through your Personal Project to help you become an increasingly self-managed and self-directed learner.
- At the end of your personal project journey, they will confirm the authenticity of your work and, through a standardization process, mark your personal project against the MYP project criteria.

You will receive information and guidance from your supervisor that includes:

- guides about the personal project
- a timetable with deadlines

- the assessment criteria for the project
- advice on how to keep and use your process journal
- the importance of personal analysis and reflection
- formative feedback
- requirements for academic honesty.

Your school will set up the supervisor process, allocations and the sharing of personal project guiding information in ways that best suit your school context.

How can your Personal Project supervisor provide support, collaboration and feedback?

Your responsibility: Organizing the meeting

Employing your communication, media literacy and social skills you need to contact your supervisor for an appropriate and regular time to meet. Your meetings are a time for you to share your ideas and progress, collaboratively discuss these ideas and your progress, and for your supervisor to provide you with feedback.

Once a time has been confirmed along with a location, make sure you send your supervisor a meeting request so this meeting is added to their busy calendars.

Ensure you come prepared and ready to share, reflect and receive feedback. Your process journal needs to be present at your personal project meetings. Make sure you take notes and document each meeting in your process journal as evidence of your communication and social skills.

Supervisor's responsibility: Engaging in the meeting

At your meetings with your supervisor they will ask you how you are progressing and read through, or listen to, sections of your process journal. They will give you feedback and guidance based on what you have shared with them and ensure that you have the tools to go further.

A great tool to provide your supervisor with at the personal project meetings is the GROWTH model question starters. These question starters will help you analyse just where you are currently in your personal project at the time of the meeting, break down what needs to happen and help you set goals as a result of the support, collaboration and feedback your supervisor has given you.

G – Goals: What do you need to achieve?

R – Reality: What is happening now?

O – Options: What could you do?

W – Will: What will you do?

T – Tactics: How and when will you do it?

H – Habits: How will you sustain your success?

Make sure you connect with your supervisor regularly and reflect on your meetings and interactions with them in your process journal. Remember, your supervisor is your one-person cheer squad throughout the process of the personal project; analyse take their ideas and feedback on board and grow as an increasingly effective communicator and self-managed learner throughout the process.

Managing the process and your time

Tips for successfully managing your time:

1 Create a realistic plan.

2 Re-evaluate throughout. Does your plan need adjusting? Are some tasks taking more or less time than you anticipated?

3 Checklists can help you keep track of your progress:

	Started?	**Completed?**
Decide on a topic/subject for your project	✔	✔
Goal statement	✔	✔
Set your objectives/outcome	✔	✔
Start your process journal	✔	
Meeting with supervisor	✔	
Complete your research		
Take action		
Start writing report		

4 Remember to take breaks every now and then.

CHAPTER 9

Managing the process and your time

ATL skills

- Organization skills
- Affective skills

LEARNER PROFILE ATTRIBUTES

Principled

Caring

Balanced

Growing as a balanced learner requires intentional planning, reflection and organization. Balanced learners understand the importance of balancing the different aspects of our lives – intellectually, physically and emotionally – to achieve well-being for ourselves and others.

As students in your final year of the MYP there are no doubt multiple commitments and responsibilities that require your focus and time:

- school
- homework
- study for examinations
- clubs
- sporting groups
- part-time work
- community engagement

Just to name a few …

And of course, time with family, friends, pursuing hobbies and side projects, engaging in various social media platforms and relaxing downtime to recharge is of utmost importance and needs to be considered and prioritized.

In MYP Year 5, added to this list is the personal project.

These can require a significant amount of juggling and can become overwhelming if not managed wisely.

A tool to support you and ensure that you do not become overwhelmed is to prioritize just what is required of you. Prioritization is a skill that requires reflection and planning ahead.

KEY WORD

Prioritize is a verb, an action word. To prioritize is something you need to actively do. To prioritize means to determine the order that you will address just what is required of you. Prioritizing your workload is a continual, reflective process.

One way of helping you prioritize and manage the Personal Project process and time is through "to do" lists. To do lists are such a simple and yet effective means of organizing the various aspects of your life and the process of your Personal Project.

Choose strategic points throughout the process, (this may be each week, fortnightly, monthly, it is up to you) and consider your prioritization needs when you choose these strategic points. Use a planning method that best suits your approach to learning, for example a diary, an online calendar with set notifications and reminders or, your chosen planning method from Chapter 3. It is important that the planning method you choose is your preferred planning method that you are comfortable with.

Using this planning method, create your to do list by simply jotting down in bullet point form what you need to achieve within the time frame you have set. Once you have jotted this down, allocate a numerical prioritization order or highlight the most important to least important to help you visualize and organize just what you need to achieve.

Make sure you include strategic meeting times with your Personal Project supervisor so you can receive the best possible support and further develop your social and communication skills.

Tick these off as you complete each of these tasks, as this will help you remain positive and continual bursts of accomplishment will help you effectively engage in the personal project all the way through to the end.

Key to personal project success is prioritizing your workload. Forward planning and prioritization means you won't leave the personal project to the last minute and consequently experience the unnecessary stress and become overwhelmed.

Remember to pause every once in a while; close or shut down your devices and head outdoors or to a quite location to unwind, rest your body and mind and recharge. Take the time to reflect, be mindful and be still. Time to pause is crucial to effectively managing your process and time as this demonstrates how you are growing as a balanced learner who understands the importance of balancing the intellectual, physical and emotional aspects of your life.

CHAPTER SUMMARY KEY POINTS

- The personal project is an ongoing piece of work, so you need to manage your time well.
- Re-evaluate your priorities throughout the process.
- Create a checklist of tasks so you can keep track of what you have completed, and what still needs to be done.
- Remember to take time out every now and then.

The moderation process

EXTERNAL MODERATION

After being marked by your teacher, your work will be sent to the IB for external moderation.

DOCUMENTS

You will need to send the following documents to the IB:

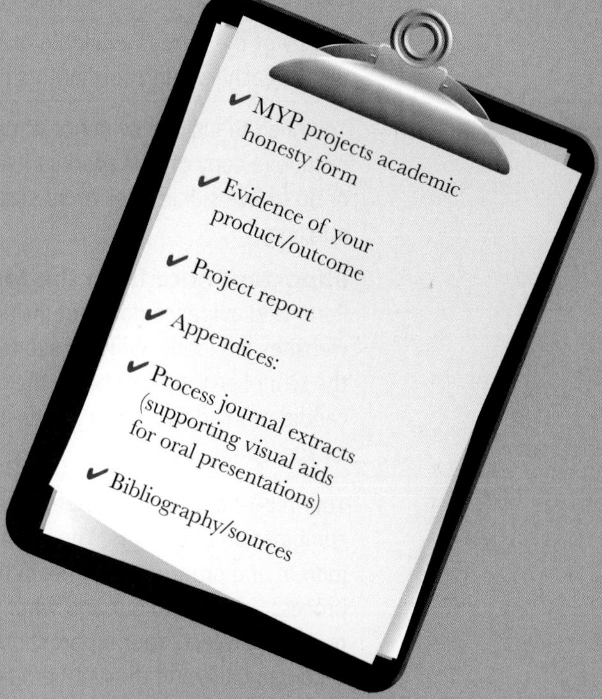
✔ MYP projects academic honesty form
✔ Evidence of your product/outcome
✔ Project report
✔ Appendices:
✔ Process journal extracts (supporting visual aids for oral presentations)
✔ Bibliography/sources

DETERMINING YOUR GRADE

The moderators will use these documents to determine your final grade.

CHAPTER 10

The moderation process

After your project is internally marked within your school, it will be submitted to the IB for external moderation. This is to ensure accuracy and consistency of marking across all IB World Schools.

MYP teachers and programme coordinators around the world serve as IB moderators. They receive training and support to ensure a consistent standard of marking is upheld. Some of your own teachers may well be moderators. To avoid conflicts of interest, the IB does not assign moderators to schools that they have associations with.

Personal project moderation process components

As part of the moderation process, you must submit the following components:

MYP projects academic honesty form	You will need this form from the beginning of your project since you must complete three sections during meetings with your supervisor. A copy of the form is available to schools on the MyIB website which teachers and coordinators have access to.
Evidence of your product/outcome	You need to include evidence of the product/outcome. You can include (a copy of) the product itself, or extracts of the product, or up to five still images or 30 seconds of video of the product/outcome. **Important note from the May 2017 subject report:** Permitted evidence does not include URL links to product/outcome websites or videos, which if submitted must not be marked by the school and will not be by the examiner. To provide evidence candidates should submit screenshots, screen casts, or video files, as appropriate.
Project report	Your report can be written, electronic, oral, visual or a combination of formats. The report is distinct from your process journal and product/outcome. In the report, you discuss the process you carried out and what you learnt from completing the personal project. Your report should be structured in identifiable sections, following the MYP projects objectives.
Appendices: Process journal extracts Supporting visual aids for oral presentations	These are short sections from your process journal that exemplify the knowledge, processes and skills you developed through the project. If your report is an oral presentation, you may include the visual aids you used, but they will count towards the ten A4 pages or (annotated) screenshots you can submit in the appendices.
Bibliography/sources	You must include a bibliography that follows a recognized convention appropriate for the task. You may use in-text citations, footnotes/endnotes or other recognized systems to credit the ideas of others in your work.

Determining your grade

Once your project is moderated, your overall grade will be calculated. To arrive at your final grade, the levels for each criterion will be added together and then converted to a 1–7 overall grade. Grade boundaries, along with a general grade descriptor, for each MYP level are included below. **Please note that grade boundaries are subject to change each year after the moderation process.**

Grade	Boundary guidelines	Descriptor
1	0–3	Produces work of a very limited quality. Conveys many misunderstandings of the process of learning independently. Very rarely demonstrates critical or creative-thinking. Very inflexible, rarely shows evidence of knowledge or skills.
2	4–6	Produces a report of limited quality. Communicates limited understanding of the process of learning independently. Demonstrates limited evidence of critical or creative-thinking. Limited evidence of transfer of knowledge or approaches to learning skills into the project.
3	7–12	Produces a report of an acceptable quality in response to the selected global context. Communicates basic understanding of the process of learning independently through the project. Begins to demonstrate some basic critical and creative-thinking. Begins to transfer knowledge and approaches to learning skills into the project.
4	13–16	Produces a good-quality report in response to the selected global context. Communicates basic understanding of the process of learning independently through all stages of the cycle of inquiry. Often demonstrates critical and creative-thinking. Transfers some knowledge and some approaches to learning skills into the project.
5	17–21	Produces a generally high-quality report that demonstrates a thorough process in response to the selected global context. Communicates good understanding of the process of learning independently through all stages of the cycle of inquiry. Demonstrates critical and creative-thinking, sometimes with sophistication. Usually transfers knowledge and approaches to learning skills into the project.
6	22–25	Produces a high-quality report that demonstrates an occasionally innovative process in response to the selected global context. Communicates extensive understanding of the process of learning independently through all stages of the cycle of inquiry. Demonstrates critical and creative-thinking, frequently with sophistication. Transfers knowledge and approaches to learning skills into the project.
7	26–32	Produces a high-quality report that demonstrates a thorough and innovative process in response to the selected global context. Communicates comprehensive, nuanced understanding of the process of learning independently through all stages of the cycle of inquiry. Consistently demonstrates sophisticated critical and creative-thinking. Successfully transfers knowledge and approaches to learning skills into the project with independence.

CHAPTER SUMMARY KEY POINTS

- After being internally marked, your Personal Project will be externally moderated by the IB.
- You must submit the following components for moderation:
  - MYP projects academic honesty form
  - evidence of your product/outcome
  - project report
  - appendices (including process journal extracts)
  - bibliography/sources.
- Your final 1–7 grade is calculated based on the total levels you receive for each of the four criteria.

Appendices

TIPS FOR A SUCCESSFUL PERSONAL PROJECT

Top 10 tips from students

1 Just start. Start as soon as you can. Do not leave it until the last minute. – BS, Good Shepherd Lutheran College

2 The PP is *very* long and intensive so make sure you are doing it on something you are genuinely interested in and care about, so that you remain dedicated to the project for the whole eight months and don't lose interest in it. That way it doesn't become a drag but rather something fun that you can do on a topic you are really passionate about. – JC-H, Southbank International School

3 It is a good idea to choose a topic that you are not an expert in already. By discovering new things through inquiry and creating the product/outcome you will be more challenged and not just rely on what you already know. – TZ, Good Shepherd Lutheran College

4 For my personal project goal I chose something really personal to me. My best friend was undergoing chemotherapy at the time, so as a way to show my support for her and help myself come to terms with what was happening I chose to use my painting skills to depict her experiences. By choosing this goal I was able to not only grow as an artist, but also to support my friend and help us process what was happening. – Anonymous

5 I chose to use my personal project as a way of exploring possible career choices. I have wanted to pursue a career in early childhood education when I finish school so my personal project goal was to create a child's sensory learning book. From all the inquiry, testing and observations with children that went into making this book, I was sure that the subjects I chose in the following year would be ones that led me down the path to a university qualification in early childhood education. The personal project confirmed the career path I wanted to take. – AB, Good Shepherd Lutheran College

6 Focus your process journal around the ATLs you apply, making sure you have a minimum of one entry that clearly applies to each. This is extremely helpful when using them as evidence for your report. – FY, Southbank International School

7 When writing your personal project report it is essential that you include the ATLs and IB learner profile traits you have developed. When you do that, the person grading it will see the importance of your project on the community and will see straight away whether it is reflective of an IB student, allowing you a better chance of reaching the top levels of the criteria. – ZS, Southbank International School

8 You need to balance your efforts between the product and the process journal and report. The product itself is only worth a twelfth of your final mark, so you should invest more time in perfecting your entries and the report, where most of the evidence of the criteria will be found. – GdB, Southbank International School

9 Make sure you take notes during your supervisor meetings. My supervisor was able to help me organize my project and get me to where I needed to be when I was getting stuck and a bit lost. – JB, Good Shepherd Lutheran College

10 Don't take it personally if your supervisor gives you advice on how to improve; criticism isn't always negative. Their job is to help you achieve the best possible level. – Anonymous

Top 10 tips from the authors

1 Choose a topic that interests you – and that can sustain your interest for the next several months.

2 Choose a topic that will allow you to learn something new. The Personal Project is a unique opportunity for you to be in control of your own learning, so take advantage of it!

3 Block out a set time each week to work on your project: for example 15 minutes each evening, a couple of hours on the weekend, or during a free period or break in the school day. Since the project is largely self-directed, it will be up to you to remain focused and motivated. Having a set time each week to focus on the project will help you to manage your time.

4 Keep your supervisor informed of key developments in your project – and of any challenges you may face. It is your supervisor's job to support you in the process, but that does not mean taking the initiative for you.

5 When researching, it is beneficial to ensure you keep an accurate record of the sources you have accessed. Online programs such as Diigo are beneficial and can help you generate a list of sources. Check with your school's Librarian – they are experts when it comes to research and academic honesty.

6 From little things big things grow. Although at first the Personal Project can seem like a significant challenge, if you plan well and simply get stuck into it, very soon you will see your project grow from its small beginnings into the significant project it is meant to be.

7 Make sure your process journal is an ever growing and evolving document. Use this as a way to really show your process and make your thinking visible for others.

8 Gather specific feedback from mentors, teachers, friends, family and experts in the topic you have chosen.

9 Remember to plan ahead carefully, think of multiple options and think ahead considering all your other responsibilities. You are managing a significant project and this takes careful planning and goal setting.

10 Have fun! It's easy to get distracted by the fact that the personal project is an assessment – the word "assessment" alone can often strike fear into the hearts of students. But don't forget that the personal project is an opportunity to engage in a sustained inquiry of *a topic that interests you* (see Tip number 1). You will get out of the personal project exactly what you put into it. If you approach the task with a positive mindset, you will reap the rewards.

PERSONAL PROJECT EXAMPLE REPORT 1

Project summary

The student created a web site focused on the issue of global warming.

NOTE: Only the project report is included here. The appendix, including process journal extracts and evidence of the product (where some evidence of the criteria can be found), is not included. It is important to remember that the project is assessed holistically, which means that evidence for each criterion can be found in the process journal, the product or the report. The report that is included here is meant to give you an idea of how to format a written report, not to provide definitive evidence of each strand of the criteria. Where evidence of the criteria is included, this has been highlighted and annotated for you.

Assessment comments

Criteria	Level	Assessor's comments
Criterion A: Investigating	8	This work achieved level 8 because the student: i defined a clear and highly challenging goal and context, considering the many layers to the context that she chose (globalization and sustainability) ii identified prior learning and subject-specific knowledge iii demonstrated excellent research skills through a detailed bibliography and references to some of her sources in the report.
Criterion B: Planning	8	This work achieved level 8 because the student: i developed rigorous, measurable criteria for the product/outcome ii presented a detailed and accurate plan of the development process of the project, especially in the process journal iii demonstrated excellent self-management skills.
Criterion C: Taking action	8	This work achieved level 8 because the student: i created an excellent product/outcome in response to the goal, global context and criteria. ii demonstrated excellent thinking skills through detailed use of the process journal iii demonstrated excellent communication and social skills.

Evidence of this strand is not very explicit in the report. The process journal (not included here) includes evidence of prior learning and subject-specific knowledge in the form of mind maps, notes, reflections, etc. The product itself also includes evidence of this strand.

Evidence of these strands of the criteria are present within the process journal, which is not included here.

Most of the evidence of this criterion is included in the product itself and the process journal, which are not included with this report example.

Criterion D: Reflecting	8	This work achieved level 8 because the student: i presented an excellent evaluation of the product/outcome against her criteria ii presented excellent reflection on how completing the product extended her knowledge of and understanding of the topic and global context iii presented excellent reflection on her development as an IB learner through the project.

Changing Tides

The causes of global warming, its impacts on coastal areas, and potential mitigation action

MYP Personal Project

PROJECT CONTENTS

Criterion A: Investigating, **i**: define a clear goal and global context for the project, based on personal interests.

I have given the precise meaning of the goal of my project, I have explained how my topic connects to my personal interests. I have described what makes the project personal: my experiences, my interests and ideas that make it important to me.

1. INVESTIGATING

1.1 Project topic

Global warming is a pressing issue, which could potentially have catastrophic impacts on our fragile planet and on future generations. I profoundly believe that it is impossible to mitigate the effects of global warming on humanity unless everyone has a basic understanding of the problem, its causes, and its effects.

I spent part of my childhood living in the Netherlands, a beautiful country characterised by its flat and extremely low geography – almost 30 percent of its land is actually below sea level. A preponderance of the area of the Netherlands consists of polders, which are pieces of land that, with the help of ingenious engineering, have been reclaimed and held back from the North Sea. Dikes, canals, pumping station; the Dutch have done everything to stop the sea from eating back their land. With emissions of greenhouse gases reaching unprecedented levels, and the global temperatures rising irrevocably, could more and more coastal areas face the same difficulties as the Netherlands? Will we be

Criterion A i: The student begins to articulate a clear goal here. This will come into sharper focus later, when she describes the final product.

Criterion A i: I considered some possible global contexts that applied to my project and have explained their connections.

Criterion A i: I have defined the global context that applies best to my project and have explained its connection.

Criterion A i: If I made changes to my goal during the project, I have explained the changes and why I made them.

able to limit global warming before the seas destroy our low-lying coastline? If so, how? I chose this topic so that I could find answers to these questions, and share them with anyone who might be interested; because, as the late Nelson Mandela perspicaciously stated, "education is the most powerful weapon which you can use to change the world."

Once I had identified an area I was interested in, I developed a more concrete and concise personal project topic: *the causes of global warming, its impacts on coastal areas, and potential mitigation action*. This distinctive definition of my topic guided me through the investigating, planning and creating stages of my Personal Project.

This topic could be investigated through the filter of almost all of the global contexts; however, the most appropriate were undoubtably Orientation in space and time, Globalisation and sustainability and Scientific and technical innovation (see appendix 1). By approaching this topic from the concepts of Orientation in space and time, I could have analysed how changes in climate have affected the migration and population dynamics throughout history, and how global warming can affect the movement of individuals and societies in the future. Additionally, this global context would have allowed me to investigate with more detail into the history of our climate, as well as the local and global perspectives on the importance of protecting coastal areas and mitigating the impacts of global warming.

If I had focused on Globalisation and sustainability, the scope of my investigation would have included how global decision-making impacts the environment, and the rate at which mitigation actions are implemented on a national/international scale. Furthermore, I could have inquired into how globalisation and the growth of multinational industries has contributed to anthropogenic global warming.

Naturally, out of the six major global contexts, Scientific and technical innovation was the most apt for the topic I had chosen. This global context would enable me to probe into how global warming affects human activity, how human and natural systems interact, and how human activity could affect or alter the laws of nature. In addition to this, through the lens of this global context, I could look at how we can use our understanding of simple and complex scientific principles to develop ways of mitigating the impacts of global warming and rising sea levels, and analyse how technical innovation is being, or could potentially be, used to solve this critical environmental issue.

Initially, I planned to present my findings regarding the topic in the form of a research report (an outline of the report can be found in appendix 3). As a supplement to the report, I also planned on creating a Prezi presentation (or a presentation with a similar visual complement), which would outline the material and research included in the report, placing a specific emphasis on the causes of global warming, and what we can do to decrease the acuteness of its impacts. By presenting my research to an audience, I hoped to reach out to the general public, educating them on what the problem is and, most importantly, on what we can do on an individual scale to mitigate the effects of global warming.

My original idea of producing a research report and presentation, eventually evolved into the idea of creating a website. This allowed me to present my research in a more interactive, two-way format, enabling me to reach out to a larger audience, and thus enhancing the educational element of the project. A website is not as static as a report or a presentation; it can change and be moulded by new research and new data, and it allows the users to investigate into the aspect of my research that most interests them. Producing a website as my final outcome contributed greatly to the development of my information literacy and communication skills, as I had never used an online medium to present and exhibit my work before. Creating a website stretched me out and beyond of my comfort zone, and this made the development of my product marvellously satisfying.

Criterion A: Investigating, **iii:** demonstrate research skills.

I have identified what I already knew about this topic/project and the sources of my knowledge.

1.2 Selection of sources

The first source I referred to was a statement made by the American Association for the Advancement of Science (2009), ratified by 18 of the world's leading scientific associations and environmental organisations (see appendix 6). This statement of consensus amongst the heads of climate science regarding the causes of global warming, proved to be pivotal to the refinement and narrowing of my research and goal. The document states that, "observations throughout the world make it clear that climate change is occurring, and rigorous scientific research demonstrates that the greenhouse gases emitted by human activities are the primary driver." From this passage, I extracted three key points that I wanted to expand on with my research: (1) evidence that global warming is occurring, (2) the impacts of greenhouse gases, (3) how human activities are responsible for the emission of greenhouse gases. The document also states that the impacts of global warming "include sea level rise for coastal states", and further asserts that "if we are to avoid the most severe impacts of climate change, emissions of greenhouse gases must be dramatically reduced." From this, I obtained two more crucial research topics: the relationship between global warming and sea level rise, and how greenhouse gas emissions can be reduced. Overall, this source provided me with a synoptic outline of the content I had to learn more about.

The resources that I found most useful throughout the project were the IPCC Fifth Assessment Reports and other technical papers by the IPCC published by the Cambridge University Press. (Refer to appendix 6 for an in-depth evaluation of this source). These reports provided authoritative, accurate, current and objective information on the progression of global warming and rising sea levels. From these reports, I sourced the vast majority of the facts and figures I referred to in my website.

Another source I found useful was Professor Lord Tony Giddens' lecture entitled *The Politics of Climate Change 2014: What Cause for Hope?* (Read more about the lecture in appendix 8). This lecture reinforced the idea that proactivity is key, and that by educating the public we can move one step closer towards solving the issue of global warming. Attending this lecture made it clear to me that creating a website would be the best way of drawing the general public closer to this environmental problem, as to ensure that everyone is taking action. Another lecture I attended was entitled *Accelerating the Transition to a Fossil-fuel-free Future* and was held at Imperial College by Professor Sir David King. This lecture was also very informative as it dealt with the issue of global warming from a different perspective, specifically looking at the correlation between energy demand, crude oil production and anthropogenic CO_2 emissions. This lecture was particularly useful as it outlined the major energy sources and the government's role in making the transition to renewables.

In addition to these sources, I also frequently consulted online databases (such as the World Bank), and other online resources. I always ensured that the information I was gathering from the web came from qualified sources, and that it was relevant, recent and objective.

Evidence of strands ii and ii of Criterion B are included in the process journal extracts (not included here).

2 PLANNING

2.1 Project goal

The initial goal of my Personal Project was *to produce a detailed report and a presentation on the causes of global warming, its impact on coastal areas, and current, as well as future (potential), mitigation plans and solutions to this global environmental problem.* This goal was based on my original aim of compiling a research report (and presentation) to demonstrate my findings; I had to amend this goal when I decided to change my product to a website.

Criterion A i: I have expanded on my goal here. This is further evidence of Criterion A, strand **i**.

The finalised version of my Personal Project goal was less wordy, and more to the point: to produce a website to educate the public about the causes of global warming, its impacts on coastal areas, and potential mitigation action. This goal encompasses all the features that define my project: it takes the form of a website; it has an educative purpose; it includes information about the causes of global warming, how this phenomenon affects low-lying coastal areas, and potential mitigation action that could be implemented. This goal was definitely challenging and demanding, as it required all of the key ATL skills, and combined creativity and logic, in a new, unfamiliar way. Nevertheless, I knew that if I remained focused and determined, this goal would be achievable.

To achieve this goal I planned to use the information I had gathered from an array of sources in the investigation stage, to create relevant and coherent content for the pages of my website. The central aim of my project was researching, and educating myself on the causes and impacts of global warming; producing a website was not a priority, but rather a medium through which I could transfer the knowledge I had acquired to the public in an intelligible and appealing way. Because of this, I decided that there was no use in spending all my time creating my own HTML code from scratch; I chose to use an only HTML editor called wix.com, a website which allows you to easily create an appealing website for free. However, I still wanted to exhibit my creative skills, and therefore I decided not to rely on any predetermined template provided by the platform; instead, I defined my own theme, and designed the format, structure and features of each page of the website myself.

Criterion B: Planning, **i**: develop criteria for the product/outcome.

I have developed rigorous, measurable criteria for the product. I explain in more detail how she will measure the success of my product against the criteria in my process journal extracts (not included here); this includes audience surveys to measure the qualitative aspect, for example.

2.2 Success criteria

Once I had settled on a definitive goal for my personal product, I started developing an adequate set of criteria, which I could use in due course to evaluate the success of my project. These criteria, comprising details relating to the form, function, audience and cost of my project, are outlined in the table below. For the list of success criteria I had created for the research report and presentation, refer to appendix 3.

Goal	To produce a website to educate the public about the causes of global warming, its impacts on coastal areas, and potential mitigation action
Global context	Scientific and technical innovation
Form	My project will be presented as a website, created using an online HTML editor. It will contain a home page, and at least three other main pages dedicated to the causes of global warming, sea level rise and mitigation action.

2.3 Global context

As was mentioned earlier, I decided to focalise my project through the global context of Scientific and technical innovation. Because this global context combines and integrates many concepts, I started by separating it into a series of key principles and noting how they would be addressed through my personal project. This allowed me to fully comprehend the implications of the global context, as to successfully incorporate it into the project, instead of leaving it as an add-on. (Refer to appendix 2 for a schematic breakdown of Scientific and technical innovation.)

The first aspect of Scientific and technical innovation is exploring the patterns and laws of the natural world, and I decided to expand on this concept by inquiring into historical changes in temperature and natural warming patterns, and further analysing the scientific principles behind the greenhouse effect. To evaluate the interaction between human and natural systems, I chose to inquire into the sources of anthropogenic greenhouse gas emissions, and how human activity is contributing to global warming and rising sea levels. Furthermore, I decided to gain a deeper insight into how our understanding of global warming can help us adopt mitigation actions, and how technical advances can contribute to the reduction of greenhouse gas emissions. Additionally, I wanted to consider how the environment impacts human activity (i.e. the consequences of global mean sea level rise).

Evidence of the product (Criterion C, strand **i**) was included in the student's submission to the IB but was not included here due to privacy issues. The student's process journal, not included here, includes evidence of strands **ii** and **iii** of Criterion C.

3. TAKING ACTION

Once I had collected a significant amount of information, I set out to achieve the goal I had devised in the planning stage of the project. I had to actively work towards transferring the knowledge I had acquired to the public in a dynamic, intriguing way through my website.

Editing the format and layout of the content of each page proved to be significantly harder, and definitely more time-consuming, than I had predicted, and I found myself struggling to meet the deadlines I set for myself. With the exhibition fast approaching, it was imperative for me to find a more effcient and effective way of transferring the information I had gathered through the research stage to my website. I decided that, to accelerate the process of creating and editing each page, I would firstly type up *all* the content of the page based on the notes I took when researching. After this, I would select the images and media files that I planned to exhibit on the page to support the written content. I would then make a quick sketch, or "blueprint", of what I planned the layout of my page to be like. Lastly, I would insert the word content into the website (change the fonts, text size, alignment, etc.), and subsequently add the images and media files.

I compiled a survey, or feedback form, to determine how my website was received, and to identify areas of improvement (evidence of this feedback from and the responses that I collected can be found in appendix 4). I handed out this feedback form at the exhibition, which took place on the 3rd of December, 2014. At this stage, my website was roughly 75 percent complete, therefore the exhibition was an excellent opportunity to get feedback, as I still had time to make changes and amendments depending on the criticism I received. Overall, the responses were positive; however, they also brought light to some minor areas of improvement. From the results of the survey, I deduced that I had to include more scientific information, statistics, models and facts, as to increase the educational component of the website, and strengthen the likelihood of students using my site as a source when working on a project or assignment. Looking back at the suggestions I received, I concluded that I had to work on making the format of my pages more consistent, as this would make it easier to find information on the site.

Once it was complete, my website comprised 15 individual pages. Refer to appendix 8 for a diagram illustrating the "backbone" or structure of my website, including all the pages I created and how they are arranged.

Criterion D: Reflecting, i: evaluate the quality of the product/outcome against their criteria.

I have included a specific, quantifiable means of assessing the success of one of my criteria.

4 REFLECTING

4.1 Reflection on product

Overall, I am satisfied with what I have accomplished through this product, as I have achieved my goal and fulfilled the criteria that I outlined in the planning stage of the project. I received many positive comments at the personal project exhibition, and the results of the feedback form that I handed out revealed that all of the people who viewed my website found it professional, informative and visually appealing. In addition to this, 97 percent of the audience (9 year-olds and over) stated that they learnt something from the website, and found locating and understanding information easy, or very easy.

This indicated that, comprehensively, the product I have created complies with the criteria that I had laid out formerly, as the website generally fulfils its educative purpose, and appeals to a wide demographic range. Furthermore, although I have still not acquired my own domain, the entire process of website creation was cost-free – which was a definite advantage and part of my initial criteria.

Criterion D: Reflecting, ii: reflect on how completing the project has extended their knowledge and understanding of the topic and the global context.

I have reflected on how completing the project has extended my knowledge and understanding of my chosen topic and global context.

Nevertheless, what I found most gratifying about the personal project experience was the insight I acquired into global warming. I am now able to perceive the magnitude and relevance of this issue, and specifically, the importance of pursuing mitigation strategies both on an individual and on a global scale. Most importantly, this project enabled me to apprehend the momentousness of Scientific and Technical Innovation, and how our knowledge of the interactions between human activities and natural systems can shape the future of our planet. Furthermore, I explored various methods of data collection, and analysed historical and predictive models of natural/climatological systems, and this helped me gain a more profound understanding of the world in which we live, and how it functions. Additionally, I gained an insight on how ingenuity and scientific progress, accompanied by modernisation and innovative engineering, can generate solutions to global problems. In conclusion, this project allowed me to recognise the full extent of my innate interest in science and how it can be applied to solve imminent global problems.

4.2 Reflection on learning

Undertaking the personal project was a highly enriching and edifying experience, as it has allowed me to grow as a person and as a learner, by allowing me to introspectively assess my attributes and abilities. The project required a level of commitment and self-discipline that I had never encountered before; it stretched me as a learner, and it allowed me to augment my Approaches to Learning (ATL) skills, especially in respect to self-management, research and thinking.

Self-management is an intrinsic aspect of the personal project, as each individual must take responsibility for his/her own actions. Throughout the investigation and creation stages of the process, I had to organize my time, research and meetings with my supervisor. I met with my superior on a weekly basis, and each time we met I would record the advice she shared with me so that I could refer to them as I worked on my project. This organization technique was very constructive, as I was able to keep track of the steps I needed to take in order to complete the project to the best standard possible. Furthermore, before beginning to construct my website, I created a detailed Gantt chart (see appendix 8) delineating the tasks I had to complete each week regarding both my product (the website) and my process journal. This allowed me to set shorter "due-dates" for myself, to guide me through the process. Often, I found it diffcult to strike a functional balance between extracurricular activities, school work and personal project work, but eventually I managed to meticulously schedule my tasks as to allocate 6–10 hours per week for personal project. I had to quickly adapt to the responsibility of completing a major independent task, and to do this I developed many strategies to guide my personal project inquiry, and to help alleviate the pressure of achieving my aims in a limited amount of time. The self-management skills that I developed are transferrable to any future project, and will be a major asset for the IB Diploma Programme.

Criterion D: Reflecting, iii: reflect on their development as IB learners through the project.

I have reflected in detail on the ATL skills that I have developed throughout the project. I provide specific examples to support my points.

Through the investigation stage, I used my research and media literacy skills to locate, organize, analyse, evaluate and synthesize information from a variety of sources. I relied on data from a combination of print and digital sources, including websites, reports, newspaper articles, raw data sheets and letters, which I cited in a running bibliography. This project has changed my outlook on research, as I now know how to assess the accuracy and relevance of information, and how to process and apply data taken from both primary and secondary sources. In addition to this, I demonstrated information literacy skills as I was able to make connections between numerous different sources, and my website combined multimedia technology to form a cohesive representation of my findings.

In addition to self-management and research, I constantly saw myself applying and developing critical-thinking, creative-thinking and transfer skills. From the start of my project, I identified a project topic, and started developing aims, goals and objectives to help me produce an authentic product. I also used my critical-thinking skills to identify and overcome obstacles and challenges, and to essentially break down my goal into more manageable components. I had to quickly develop my creative-thinking skills, in order collate the knowledge I gained in an original way through my website; this required transferring familiar learning skills to unfamiliar situations.

Criterion D **iii**: I have reflected on the subject-specific knowledge that I demonstrated throughout the project – and how that knowledge developed during the process. This is not specifically mentioned in Criterion D, but this addition shows meaningful reflection as a learner.

Moreover, the research I conducted was highly interdisciplinary, and throughout the process I constantly had to draw on multiple branches of knowledge. More specifically, my topic integrated aspects of chemistry and physics, as the knowledge of these subjects helped me understand the natural and anthropogenic causes of global warming, and combined these with aspects of geography, especially in respect to how global warming affects human and environmental systems. Furthermore, this project allowed me to make the connection between scientific concepts and the language and communication skills that are needed to present them.

In addition to developing these essential ATL skills, I have also become a more inquisitive, knowledgeable, risk-taking individual, and have acquired attributes of the Learner Profile that will accompany me through life. This project has taught me to learn independently, with enthusiasm and passion, and to nurture my curiosity, channelling it through my research. I have also learnt how to develop and apply a conceptual understanding of the principles of natural and human systems, in order to evaluate and engage with issues of a global significance (namely, global warming). Finally, I now approach challenges without hesitation, but with forethought, determination, resilience and ambition; I have learnt that the greatest satisfaction can come from leaving your comfort zone, exploring new ideas, and sharing your knowledge in innovative ways.

Criterion D **iii:** **I have** demonstrated excellent reflection on myself as an IB learner, making explicit reference to the learner profile.

Criterion A **iii:**
I provided an extensive bibliography, formatted according to MLA conventions. This shows evidence of depth and breadth of research. Note this bibliography has been redacted.

5. BIBLIOGRAPHY

"About Australian Climate." About Australian Climate. N.p., n.d. Web. 10 Dec. 2014. **www.bom.gov.au/climate/about/index.shtml?bookmark=enso**.

American Association for the Advancement of Science. "Statement on Climate Change from 18 Scientific Associations (2009)." Letter to Senator. 21 Oct. 2009. American Association for the Advancement of Science. N.p., 21 Oct. 2009. Web. 12 Sept. 2014. **www.aaas.org/sites/default/files/migrate/uploads/1021climate_letter1.pdf**.

Astaiza, Randy. "11 Islands That Will Vanish When Sea Levels Rise." Business Insider. Business Insider, Inc, 12 Oct. 2012. Web. 02 Dec. 2014. **www.businessinsider.com/islands-threatened-by-climate-change-2012-10? op=1&IR=T**.

Carringdon, Damian. "Global Warming Pause Is a Mirage: The Science Is Clear and the Threat Real." The Guardian. The Guardian, 27 Sept. 2013. Web. 2 Dec. 2014.

"Causes of Climate Change." EPA. Environmental Protection Agency, n.d. Web. 08 Dec. 2014. **https://19january2017snapshot.epa.gov/climatechange_.html**.

"Changing Tides: Website Feedback" Survey. 3 December 2014.

"Climate Science Glossary." Skeptical Science. N.p., n.d. Web. 10 Dec. 2014 **www.skepticalscience.com/argument.php**.

"Climate Science Info Zone." Natural Factors: Variations in the Sun's Output – Science Museum. N.p., n.d. Web. 10 Dec. 2014. **http://whoami.sciencemuseum.org.uk/ClimateChanging/ClimateScienceInfoZone/**.

"Coastal Areas Impacts & Adaptation." EPA. Environmental Protection Agency, n.d. Web. 10 Dec. 2014. **https://19january2017snapshot.epa.gov/climate-impacts/climate-impacts-coastal-areas_.html**.

"Coastal Florida and Everglades–Sea Level Rise Map." Florida Map. N.p., n.d. Web. 10 Dec. 2014. **http://geology.com/sea-level-rise/florida.shtml**.

The Core Writing Team, IPCC Synthesis Report, Rejendra K. Pachauri, IPCC Chairman, and Leo Meyer, IPCC Head, Technical Support Unit, eds. Climate Change 2014: Synthesis Report. Rep. Vol. SYR AR5. N.p.: n.p., 2014. Print. IPCC Fifth Assessment Report.

Critchley, Emma. "Act Now to Limit Climate Change Says Climate Expert at Grantham Annual Lecture." Imperial College London. Imperial College London, 28 Nov. 2013. Web. 04 Oct. 2014. **www3.imperial.ac.uk/newsandeventspggrp/imperialcollege/naturalsciences/climatechange/newssummary/news_28-11-2013-11-8-22**.

"El Nino – An Introduction." El Nino – An Introduction. N.p., n.d. Web. 10 Dec. 2014. **http://kids.earth.nasa.gov/archive/nino/intro.html**.

Energy Efficiency and Renewable Energy. 2012 Renewable Energy Data Book. Rep. N.p.: U.S Department of Energy, 2012. Print.

"Everything You Need to Know about Earth's Orbit and Climate Change." MNN. N.p., n.d. Web. 10 Dec. 2014. **www.mnn.com/earth-matters/climate-weather/stories/everything-you-need-to-know-about-earths-orbit-and-climate- cha**.

Giddens, Anthony. "The Politics of Climate Change 2014: What Cause for Hope?" The London School of Economics and Political Science, London. 14 Oct. 2014. Lecture.

"Global Ocean Heat and Salt Content." Global Ocean Heat and Salt Content. N.p., n.d. Web. 10 Dec. 2014. **www.nodc.noaa.gov/OC5/3M_HEAT_CONTENT/**.

"The Greenhouse Effect." Greenhouse Effect: Background Material. N.p., n.d. Web. 09 Dec. 2014. **https://scied.ucar.edu/longcontent/greenhouse-effect**.

Hansen, James, Makiko Sato, and Reto Ruedy. Global Temperature Update Through 2013. Tech. N.p.: n.p., 2014. Print.

Harris, Gardiner. "Borrowed Time on Disappearing Land." The New York Times. The New York Times, 28 Mar. 2014. Web. 02 Dec. 2014.

"How Much Does Human Activity Affect Climate Change? | NCSE." How Much Does Human Activity Affect Climate Change? | NCSE. N.p., n.d. Web. 10 Dec. 2014. **http://ncse.com/climate/climate-change-101/how-much-human-responsibility-for-climate-change**.

"Ice Caps, Ice Sheets, and Ice Shelves: What's the Difference?" Exploring the Environment. N.p., n.d. Web. 10 Dec. 2014. **http://ete.cet.edu/gcc/?/ icecaps_icesheets**.

Iconfinder. N.p., n.d. Web. 14 Oct. 2014. **www.iconfinder.com/**.

"Industries We Serve – AndPlus." AndPlus RSS. N.p., n.d. Web. 10 Dec. 2014. **www.andplus.com/industries-serve/**.

IPCC Working Group I. Climate Change 2013: The Physical Science Basis. Rep. Vol. WGI AR5. N.p.: Cambridge UP, 2013. Print. IPCC Fifth Assessment Report.

Kinver, Mark. "Renewables See 'resilient Growth' in 2009." BBC News. BBC, 15 July 2010. Web. 10 Dec. 2014. **www.bbc.co.uk/news/science+environment-10646282**.

Mann, Michael E. "Volcanic Aerosols." Encyclopedia Britannica Online. Encyclopedia Britannica, n.d. Web. 10 Dec. 2014. **www.britannica.com/EBchecked/topic/235402/global-warming/274833/Volcanic-aerosols#274834**.

"Mapping Surface Temperature Changes Over Time." Class Zone. N.p., n.d. Web. 10 Dec. 2014. **www.classzone.com/books/earth_science/terc/content/investigations/esu501/esu501page06.cfm**.

"A Model of Sea Level Rise Caused by Ocean Thermal Expansion." American Meteorological Society. N.p., n.d. Web. 10 Dec. 2014. **http://journals.ametsoc.org/doi/abs/10.1175/1520-0442(1991)004%3C0438:AMOSLR%3E2.0.CO;2**.

"NASA's Earth Minute." Climate Change: Vital Signs of the Planet. N.p., n.d. Web. 10 Dec. 2014. **http://climate.nasa.gov/climate_resource_center/earthminute**.

"Nation Under Siege: Coastal Impact Study." Atom. N.p., n.d. Web. 10 Dec. 2014. **http://architecture2030.org/slr/seaside_or**.

"National Snow and Ice Data Center." Glaciers and Climate Change. N.p., n.d. Web. 10 Dec. 2014. **https://nsidc.org/cryosphere/glaciers/questions/climate.html**.

Nuccitelli, Dana. "The Wall Street Journal Denies the 97% Scientific Consensus on Human-caused Global Warming." The Guardian. N.p., 28 May 2014. Web. 10 Dec. 2014. **www.theguardian.com/environment/climate-consensus-97-per-cent/2014/may/28/wall-street-journal-denies-global-warming-consensus**.

Nudelman, Gus Lubin and Mike. "Rising Sea Levels Could Cause Staggering Damage To These Cities." Business Insider. Business Insider, Inc, 22 Apr. 2014. Web. 02 Dec. 2014. **www.businessinsider.com/cities-exposed-to-rising-sea-levels-2014-4?IR=T**.

"Oceans of Climate Change." Climate Change: Vital Signs of the Planet. N.p., n.d. Web. 10 Dec. 2014. **http://climate.nasa.gov/climate_resources/40/**.

Oreskes, Naomi. "The Scientific Consensus on Climate Change." Science AAAS. HighWire Press, n.d. Web. 09 Dec. 2014. **http://science.sciencemag.org/content/306/5702/1686**.

Pendick, Daniel. "Savage Seas." PBS. PBS, n.d. Web. 10 Dec. 2014. **www.pbs.org/wnet/savageseas/weather-side-elnino.html**.

"Rising Seas." National Geographic. N.p., n.d. Web. 10 Dec. 2014. **http://ngm.nationalgeographic.com/2013/09/rising-seas/folger-text**.

"The Role of the Ocean in Tempering Global Warming." NOAA Climate.gov. N.p., n.d. Web. 10 Dec. 2014. **www.climate.gov/news-features/blogs/enso/role-ocean-tempering-global-warming**.

"Sea Level Rise – National Geographic." National Geographic. N.p., n.d. Web. 08 Dec. 2014. **http://ocean.nationalgeographic.com/ocean/critical-issues-sea-level- rise/**.

"Sinking without Trace: Australia's Climate Change Victims." The Independent. Independent Digital News and Media, 5 May 2008. Web. 02 Dec. 2014. **www.independent.co.uk/environment/climate-change/sinking-without-trace-australias-climate-change-victims-821136.html**.

"Solar Radiation and Climate Experiment (SORCE) Fact Sheet : Feature Articles." Earth Observatory NASA. N. p., n. d. Web. 10 Dec. 2014. **http://earthobservatory.nasa.gov/Features/SORCE/**.

Solomon, S., D. Qin, M. Manning, Z. Chen, M. Marquis, K. B. Averyt, M. Tignor, and H. L. Miller, eds. Climate Change 2007: The Physical Science Basis. Rep. Vol. WGI AR4. Cambridge, United Kingdom and New York, NY, USA: Cambridge UP, 2007. Print. IPCC Fourth Assessment Report.

Tackling Global Warming. Perf. Professor Geoff Maitland and Professor Martin Trusler. Imperial College London Media Library. Imperial College London, n.d. Web. 15 Oct. 2014. **http://wwwf.imperial.ac.uk/imedia/content/view/955/tackling-global-warming**.

"10 Cities That Risk Disappearing Under Water." TheRichest. N.p., n.d. Web. 10 Dec. 2014. **http://www.therichest.com/rich-list/poorest-list/10-cities-that-risk-disappearing-under-water/2/**.

"Thermal Expansion of Sea Water Associated with Global Warming." Nature.com. Nature Publishing Group, 18 Nov. 1987. Web. 10 Dec. 2014. **http://www.nature.com/nature/journal/v330/n6144/abs/330127a0.html**.

Union of Concerned Scientists. Causes of Sea Level Rise: What the Science Tells Us. Cambridge, MA: Union of Concerned Scientists, 2013. Print.

Department of Energy. Energy Efficiency and Renewable Energy. 2012 Renewable Energy Data Book. Rep. N.p.: n.p., 2012. Print.

"U.S. Energy Information Administration – EIA – Independent Statistics and Analysis." How Much Carbon Dioxide Is Produced When Different Fuels Are Burned? N.p., n.d. Web. 10 Dec. 2014. **http://www.eia.gov/tools/faqs/faq.cfm?id=73&t=11**.

World Bank. CO_2 emissions (metric tons per capita). 2014. Raw data. Carbon Dioxide Information Analysis Center, Environmental Sciences Division, Oak Ridge National Laboratory, Tennessee, United States, n.p.

"WWF Supports IEA Conclusion: Two Thirds of Fossil Fuel Reserves Must Be Left Underground." WWF Canada -. N.p., n.d. Web. 10 Dec. 2014. **http:// www.wwf.ca/?11541/WWF-supports-IEA-conclusion-two-thirds-of-fossil-fuel-reserves-must-be-left-underground**.

PERSONAL PROJECT EXAMPLE REPORT 2

Project summary

The student learnt to play the ukulele and, using their new skills combined with their songwriting skills, write an original song and perform this accompanied solely by the ukulele.

NOTE: Only the project report is included here. The appendix, including process journal extracts and evidence of the product (where some evidence of the criteria can be found), is not included. It is important to remember that the project is assessed holistically, which means that evidence for each criterion can be found in the process journal, the product or the report. The report that is included here is meant to give you an idea of how to format a written report, not to provide definitive evidence of each strand of the criteria.

In the previous report example, where evidence of the criteria is included, this has been highlighted and annotated for you. This example has been annotated with questions as a means of provoking your thinking to peer-assess this student's work and reflect on how this report could be improved.

Think about how each section of this student's personal project could be improved. What needs to be included and what needs to be explained in further detail with examples, either within the body of the report, or the appendices?

Ukulele and Songwriting

My personal project goal is to learn to play the ukulele, then to write an original song to be accompanied by the ukulele.

MYP Personal Project

Word count: 3,217

PROJECT CONTENTS

Identify in this section of the report, how this student has presented the following:

Give the precise meaning of the goal of their project; they explain "what I wanted to achieve; when, where, how and why I wanted to achieve it".

Define the global context that applies best to their project and explain its connection.

Describe what makes their project personal: the experiences, interest and ideas that make it important to them.

If they made changes to their goal during the project, they explain the changes and why they made them.

INVESTIGATING

My personal project goal was to learn to play the ukulele, then to write a song to play on it. After creating a mind map of possible projects, I decided on something to extend my knowledge of music. I chose this as I like to perform, and this product would also help create and improve three skills I need to do so; my musical instrument ability with a ukulele, my poetic and creative ability with songwriting, and my vocal ability with singing. To achieve this I would visit Guitar Lessons Co. on Mondays and Fridays to learn to play the ukulele and record my final song, and singing lessons on Fridays and Saturdays to improve my vocals.

I chose the global context of identities and relationships as I feel this best fits my product. This context fits my project as it is about relationships, attitudes and emotions which music influences. Learning to play the ukulele and writing a song will make people feel certain ways, thus shaping their identities. This topic interests me because it will improve skills I need for performing. More than anything, I want to be an actress, and being able to play an instrument, sing and write a song looks great on an actor's resume. The skills I learnt from this project, such as how to add more techniques to my voice, will improve my everyday life too, as it will help me become a more effective communicator.

My original goal was to learn to play the ukulele and write a song to play on it, but that slightly altered. It became a goal to learn the basics of playing ukulele and to write two songs. I made these adjustments because I did not realise that in the given timeframe, I would not be able to play the instrument fluently. I also changed from one to two songs because in my first one, I didn't have my singing teacher's help. That was because I was busy preparing for my singing performance examination, and didn't have time to use my second primary source. Using the source was a requirement, and I had extra time, so I decided to create a second song.

Prior learning

Prior to starting, I knew a bit about my chosen topic. I had written poems in English and received MYP 8's, so I knew how to use techniques like rhyme, repetition and similes. These would improve how aesthetically pleasing it was to the ears and how catchy the song was. I have also had singing lessons for the past three years, so I knew a lot of techniques with vocals when I began, and how to manipulate my voice, which was helpful when recording my song.

Subject-specific knowledge

Whilst being part of the MYP programme at my school, I have taken classes that gave me knowledge I could use in my project. My Language and Literature classes from Year 7 through to Year 9 have taught me a lot about writing poetry and rhythmic prose. This knowledge helped me create my product because it meant I had the ability to write a poem, or in this case a song, that had techniques to make it catchy. Learning about this before starting my project helped me understand what techniques I should add to my song, such as rhyme, rhythm and metaphors, and their impact on the listeners.

In Year 7, I also had the Arts subjects of Music and Visual Arts. Although only brief, I learnt a bit about how music is created, and a few vocal techniques. I also learnt a bit more about stage presentation. During Visual Arts I learnt how to express myself in new ways and come up with new ideas that will interest an audience. These electives helped to give me ideas on how to please an audience, what they're looking for and how to be creative.

Identify what they already knew about this topic/project and the sources of their knowledge.

Identify what they learned in MYP subject groups before the project started, and how this was helpful.

Demonstrate research skills

Before starting my personal project I have had very limited knowledge and experience in researching. I had little knowledge on how to assess a source and format a bibliography. I knew little about primary and secondary sources, which I had picked up through Individuals and Societies and my school diary. I would just reference any site, thinking it was correct without comparing or doing anything to verify that it actually was.

Through doing this project I learnt to properly assess a source (see appendix 1). Doing this has taught me to how to verify a website, ensure I'm getting valuable and reliable information, and how to dig deeper through having research questions. This project has also taught me I can use people as a source of information, and that I need to ensure they have their facts correct, through things such as qualifications, so I'm getting correct, unbiased information. I am now able to confidently write a bibliography, and feel as though I can go online and skim through text to find the useful information.

At school, I have had many opportunities to share my research skills to peers. At lunch, when discussing the Personal Project, some of my friends have asked about the research portion of the project. I have been able to give them tips that I picked up, that they hadn't thought of, such as to skim read and check multiple websites for similar information. When in class, doing either a task or assessment, I have been able to help peers by sharing tips I have learnt through this project. I've also been able to tell them websites I have found through verifying, and been able to share information with them that I have checked through multiple sources. When some peers asked, I have also been able to show them how I set my research out, and methods I used to extract the information.

Outline the research skills they had when they started the project.

Discuss the research skills they developed through the project.

Explain how they may have shared their research skills to help peers who needed more practice.

Refer to the criteria they designed to evaluate the project product/outcome.

If they made changes to their criteria during the project, explain the changes and why they made them.

PLANNING

Level of achievement	Specification 1	Specification 2	Specification 3	Specification 4	Specification 5
Excellent 7 – 8	The song must be catchy. It must get stuck in the listener's head for at least one day.	The song is 2 to 4 minutes long. No longer, no shorter. Not even by 1 second.	No autotune is used. No vocal imperfections. Sound matches audio. Techniques are used.	There are no faults/ mistakes in strumming, chords or vocals.	The music matches the tone and lyrics well. The beat, lyrics and mood all match.
Substantial 5 – 6	The song is a bit catchy. It gets stuck in the listener's head for at least an hour.	The song is 1.20 to 4.30 minutes long. Not a second longer or shorter.	There is no autotune. One or two imperfections vocally. Techniques are used.	There are 2 to 3 mistakes in strumming, chords or vocals.	The music mostly matches the tone and lyrics. Sometimes the lyrics, mood and beat don't match.
Adequate 3 – 4	The song is a little bit catchy. Gets stuck in your head for maximum of 10 minutes.	The song is 1 to 5 minutes long. Not a minute longer or shorter.	There is a little bit of autotune. 8 or more vocal imperfections. Limited techniques.	There are 8 or more mistakes in strumming, chords or vocals.	The music only matches the tone and lyrics occasionally. Sometimes the beat, lyrics and mood match.
Limited 1 – 2	The song has under 30 seconds of catchiness. Not enjoyable to listen to.	The song is 30 seconds or less to over 5 minutes long.	Autotune is used. Lots of vocal imperfections. Limited techniques.	Consistent mistakes in strumming, chords and vocals.	The music does not match the tune and lyrics. Beat, lyrics and mood don't match.
No Evidence: 0					

Provide evidence of their planning through timelines, milestones or other tools/strategies.

Present a record of how the project progressed from start to finish.

After creating my success rubric, I created a timeline to keep track of my journey (see appendix 2). This allowed me to see the days I would be busy, the days I needed a break, and the days I could use for my project. This also helped me keep track of how often I was working on my project and how many lessons I had completed/remaining for ukulele. The calendar at the front of my process journal (see appendix 3) was also used to keep track of dates that hadn't yet occurred, but were important to remember. These included information nights at school, meetings with my supervisor and milestones such as starting the project and the completion date. This helped me remember important dates, and keep on task as I had to meet a milestone.

Outline the self-management skills they had when they started the project.

Discuss the self-management skills they developed through the project.

Explain how they may have shared their self-management skills to help peers who needed more practice.

At the start of this project, I could manage my time quite well, but not as effectively as I can now. When I began my project, I didn't use calendars or timelines to note down when I had appointments or deadlines, I just remembered them. Now, through my project, I have learnt that it's helpful to use a calendar (see appendix 3) to remember dates and times that I'm busy. I have also learnt that I need to make certain times unavailable for school, personal project, or extracurricular, and just free for myself. I find it easier to create a chart now or use a calendar that will help me know when I should be free to do my project, or other important aspects of my life. Improving this skill has helped me to balance my life.

When people ask how I manage to be busy 5–7 days a week, and still manage to do my homework/assignments and Personal Project, I can now offer advice. I tell them how I have made a timeline, and use a calendar, where I write down when I'm busy. I then divide the remaining time into a few sections: relaxing/mental and physical health, homework and the Personal Project. I then chose a time for each of these, and depending on how much schoolwork I have, I will give myself a slot to do these. I make sure I have 3–4 days for relaxing though, otherwise schoolwork takes over and I start to become sad and stressed. The few peers I have told this to have taken it on board and said they agree with the logic.

They discuss the product/outcome as the result of the process undertaken during the project.

They check that they have included evidence of their product to be submitted with the report.

TAKING ACTION

To create my product, I had to think creatively to come up with ideas for lyrics and tunes. I had to try and see things in a new light so it was entertaining, relatable and original for my audience. When I began, I could not easily think of ideas to continue my original one. Now I'm able to come up with a new idea, and make a list to continue off that (see appendix 4) so I can progress. I haven't had any opportunities to share my thinking skills with peers, especially since I don't feel confident with them.

Outline thinking skills that they had when they started the project.

Discuss thinking skills they developed through the project.

Explain how they may have shared their thinking skills to help peers who needed more practice.

When I started my project, I was lacking in communication and social skills. I would not email people to get help, or ask questions. Now I am more comfortable with talking to acquaintances, and asking for help when I am unsure. I had to improve these skills during my project as I had to contact many people for help. I gained confidence around people by talking, asking questions and being social around those I do not know. I managed to help a few people improve their social and communication skills by helping them draft emails, and helping them talk to people when they were too shy to do it by themselves at first, until they were confident enough to do it on their own.

Outline the communication and social skills they had when they started the project.

Discuss the communication and social skills they developed through the project.

Explain how they may have shared their communication and social skills to help peers who needed more practice.

When I was making my product, I had some challenges. One of these was that, when recording my second song, I was running out of time. To solve this problem, I arranged to make a one hour lesson for ukulele, instead of 30 minutes, to be more productive. Also, when I was writing my lyrics too, I couldn't think of any ideas to continue from my original. To solve this issue, I went and talked to other people, and went for a walk. I decided not to force an idea, but instead to just make a list when I got stuck of possible options. I also read over what my sources suggested I need in a song (see appendix 6), and what made the top 100 songs entertaining (see appendix 7). From this research I could begin to think of ideas to continue.

REFLECTING

Specification 1

Song 1

6/8

For this specification I gave myself a 6. I chose this as I found my song catchy, and it got stuck in my head for 6 hours, but not a whole day. To have received a higher mark, I could have gotten some more help in the creation process, and more instruments could have been used to give it a stronger beat. Also, more techniques, such as repetition, could have been used to get it stuck in the listener's head.

Song 2

6/8

I gave myself a 6 for this criteria. I feel this was right because my song got stuck in my head for a few hours at a time, and it would come to mind randomly too, but it would not stick for a day. To have improved, I could have added more of a beat, and more instruments that would have helped them, like a drum or piano. These would make the tune get stuck in people's minds.

Specification 2

Song 1

8/8

I gave myself an 8 for this criteria because my song was 2 minutes 55 seconds, well within my 3 to 4 minute criteria. I could not have improved this specification.

Song 2

8/8

I gave myself an 8 for specification 2. This song was 3 minutes 35 seconds and perfectly fit this criteria. As the time fit the limit, this could not have been improved.

Specification 3

Song 1

6/8

For this criteria, my first song scored a 6. I chose this because although there was no autotune, and vocal techniques were used, I noticed some vocal imperfections, but not many. To have improved this, I could have asked my singing teacher for help. I could also have practiced more, until the vocals were perfect.

Song 2

6/8

This song got a 6 for specification 3. I chose this because I noticed vocal mistakes. There were not a lot of them, no autotune was used, and techniques were used, so I found this mark suitable. I could have practiced to a schedule, instead of just lessons, and watched videos to learn to do more techniques vocally, to have improved.

Evaluate the product/outcome against the criteria they designed.

Identify the strengths, weaknesses and possible improvements of the product/outcome.

Specification 4

Song 1

6/8

This song received a 6 in this criteria. I chose this because, although there were only a few, I noticed vocal and strumming mistakes. If I had practiced more, for example 10 minutes, 3 times a day, I could have improved my skills and minimised errors.

Song 2

5/8

I decided to give myself a 5 for this as I noticed some vocal and strumming errors. Also, as I had limited time to record, I had to stick with what was already recorded. If I had another opportunity to record, I could have improved my song. I also could have practiced some more to eliminate the mistakes made.

Specification 5

Song 1

8/8

I gave myself an 8 for this criteria because I felt that the tone, mood, beat and lyrics or my song all matched as they were quite negative and sad. I do not think I could have improved this.

Song 2

7/8

I decided to give myself a 7 for this specification. I chose this because, although it has an empowering message, parts of the song appeared sad. Apart from that, it fit together. To have improved, I could have checked that all elements matched.

Identify challenges and the solutions they developed to meet them.

Demonstrate a deeper knowledge and understanding of their topic and the identified global context.

Base my reflection on evidence, including my process journal.

Some challenges I experienced during this project was stress and creative block. To fix these, I needed time to myself. To help stress, I had to take time away from schoolwork to have fun, and to exercise. These helped to calm me and get me back on track. I also experienced creative block. To fix this, I went outside, and did not force an idea. I talked to people for help and ideas, and this gave me inspiration.

By completing my product, I have greatly expanded my knowledge. On the topic of ukulele and singing, I have learnt a lot. I learnt how to better control and utilize my voice, and how to apply that knowledge to my creations. I can now easily add techniques, such as twang, when singing and talking. With ukulele, I now know how to write chords, and what bars are. I understand how to strum and make a strumming pattern, as well as move my fingers from chord to chord quickly. I have also learnt to add them to chords to create a song. This made me aware of all the hard work that goes into producing a song.

Completing my project has taught me a lot, and extended my knowledge about the global context I chose, "Identities and relationships". Creating my songs, especially writing the lyrics, taught me a lot about myself and how I see the world. It made me realise how I feel about my life, others and the world around me. This also helped me become aware of how others live their lives, such as their values and relationships. I noticed these things, and learnt from them, because I was trying to create lyrics and ideas, so I talked to and observed my friends. Becoming more in touch with myself and those around me has given me a greater understanding of the global context "Identities and relationships".

Identify how they have developed as a learner (using the IB learner profile as appropriate).

Discuss their strengths and weaknesses in completing the project.

Summarize the impact the project could have on their future learning.

During this process, I developed as an IB learner. One example of an IB learner profile that I developed was "Inquirer". I developed this by asking a lot of questions, doing research and extracting information. This project made me improve this skill because I had to do these things often, so I got used to doing them, and became more aware of what makes a good source (see appendix 1). Knowing that I also had to utilise and apply the information afterwards encouraged me to ask more questions and make sure I have transferred the information correctly. This project taught me to be an inquirer as I can now reference and verify sources; something I didn't do well before. I was never confident with asking questions and researching, but now that I have done this multiple times, I am finding it easier.

I also improved my profile of being a "balanced" learner. Completing this has taught me to balance my physical and mental health, and my non-academics. I also learnt how important it was that they were balanced for my well being and those around me. At the start, all of my extracurriculars with homework and assignments were stressing me. Although I am still stressed, especially since the workload has increased, I now understand when I need time off, how to prioritise, and how important this is for my well being. I can balance different aspects of my life better now.

Bibliography

"4 tips to Switch Guitar Chords Faster" **www.ultimate-guitar.com/lessons/the_guide_to/4_tips_to_switch_guitar_chords_faster.html** [accessed 05/09/15] – Secondary Source 12

"About Me" **http://completeukulele.blogspot.com.au/p/about-me.html** [accessed 20/06/15] – Secondary Source 2

Atherton. S 'Guitar Lessons Coach'

Bartley P. 'Essington School of Music' Vocal Teacher

'Complete Ukulele Chord Charts' **http://ukuchords.com/ukulele-chord-charts/** [accessed 20/06/15]

'How to Change Ukulele Strings' **http://sites.google.com/site/islandukuleleclub/uke-web-resources/how-to-determine-strumming-pattern-for.html** [accessed 08/07/15]

'How to determine the strumming pattern in songs' **https://justinguitarcommunity.com/index.php?topic=27227.0** [accessed 22/08/15]

'How to Sing and Play Ukulele at the Same Time' **www.ukuleletricks.com/how-to-sing-and-play-ukulele-at-the-same-time/** [accessed 05/09/15]

'Probing Question: What makes a song catchy?' **https://news.psu.edu/story/141354/2006/06/05/research/probing-question-what-makes-song-catchy** [accessed 05/09/15]

'What makes a song 'catchy'–science explains' **http://zmescience.com/research/studies/what-makes-a-song-catchy-science-explains** [accessed 01/10/15]

Index